# ROYAL BOROUGH OF GREENWICH

Paul Millmore worked as a freelance conservation consultant and for East Sussex County Council as Countryside Officer. For more than 30 years he was involved with the conservation of the special landscape of the South Downs and he was a leading campaigner in the creation of the South Downs National Park in 2011.

*titles published in this series*

Offa's Dyke Path South
Offa's Dyke Path North
Cleveland Way
The Ridgeway
Pennine Way
Pembrokeshire Coast Path
South Downs Way
North Downs Way
Yorkshire Wolds Way
Peddars Way and Norfolk Coast Path
Hadrian's Wall Path

Thames Path in the Country
Thames Path in London
Pennine Bridleway: Derbyshire to
    the South Pennines
Cotswold Way

**South West Coast Path**

Minehead to Padstow
Padstow to Falmouth
Falmouth to Exmouth
Exmouth to Poole

OFFICIAL NATIONAL
TRAIL GUIDE

# *South Downs Way*

## Paul Millmore

**A**urum

in association with

NATURAL
ENGLAND

# Acknowledgements

My thanks go to all the staff of the National Park and the three county councils along the Way, but particularly to Andy Gattiker, Bill Jenman, Phil Belden, Alan Stevens, Nigel Kitchener, Andrew Woodcock, David Marshall, Paul Smith, Tony Appicella, Colin Piper, Elaina Whittaker-Slark and Bill Bide. Also to the regional tourist boards, the South Downs Society (formerly the Society of Sussex Downsmen), John Dakin, Peter Brandon, John Boardman, Natural England (formerly Nature Conservancy Council), Walter and Vivien Long, Alison Bullar, Mary Parker, Glynn and Adie Jones and Chris Fairbrother. Special thanks go to Linda Bacon, Debby Emery and Romy Luffman, who all helped with the typing. Thanks also to my daughter Tamsin, my son Josh and my wife Bridget for keeping me company along parts of the route and for putting up with me during the writing of the book.

This book is dedicated to Gideon and Rowan Millmore who journeyed with me in spirit. *Paul Millmore*

*Paul Millmore was walking and cycling the South Downs Way for the revisions to this book only months before his untimely death from cancer in March 2012. He was also continuing to campaign for improvements to the countryside, marine and built environment in the newly created South Downs National Park. His vision, energy and commitment to all things environmental will be sorely missed.*

This fully revised and updated edition first published in 2012 by Aurum Press Ltd
7 Greenland Street, London NW1 0ND • www.aurumpress.co.uk
in association with Natural England
www.naturalengland.org.uk • www.nationaltrail.co.uk

First published in 2003
Text copyright © 1990, 1996, 1999, 2001, 2004, 2008, 2010, 2012 by Paul Millmore

Pictures are copyright © the photographer/agency and are by: pp. 19, 20–21, 25, 28, 30–31, 34, 44 (bottom), 45 (top), 48, 53, 74–75, 80, 85, 98, 112, 128–29 (top) and 136 Martin Page; 16 Andy Gattiker; 1, 2–3, 13, 14–15, 22, 36, 38, 43, 45 (bottom), 50, 52, 55, 56, 58, 62, 66 (top and middle), 67, 72, 78, 83, 84, 88, 90–91, 92, 95, 100–101, 102, 106, 108, 110, 114–15, 118, 121, 122 (top and bottom), 127, 128, 130, 132, 134–35, 138, 140, 143 and 151 Alamy; 60–61 Rob Allchin shutterclutter.co.uk; 65 Michael Lank; 12 Trailblaze; 40 National Trust images; 44 (top) National Maritime Museum, Greenwich, London; 71 Mirrorpix; 66 (bottom) The Granger Collection/TopFoto.

**OS Ordnance Survey** This product includes mapping data licensed from Ordnance Survey® with the permission of the Controller of Her Majesty's Stationery Office. © Crown copyright 2012. All rights reserved. Licence number 43453U.

Ordnance Survey and Travelmaster are registered trademarks and the Ordnance Survey symbol and Explorer are trademarks of Ordnance Survey, the national mapping agency of Great Britain.

ISBN 978 1 78131 088 5
1 3 5 7 9 10 8 6 4 2
2013 2015 2017 2016 2014

Book design by Robert Updegraff • Printed in China
Cover photograph: *View of Kingston Ridge on the South Downs from Lewes*
Half-title-page: *View from Ditchling Beacon, South Downs National Park*
Title-page: *Paragliders at Devil's Dyke*

Aurum Press want to ensure that these National Trail Guides are always as up to date as possible – but stiles collapse, pubs close and bus services change all the time. If, on walking this path, you discover any important changes of which future walkers and riders need to be aware, do let us know. Either email us on **trailguides@aurumpress.co.uk** with your comments, or if you take the trouble to drop us a line to:

**Trail Guides, Aurum Press, 7 Greenland Street, London NW1 0ND,**
we'll send you a free guide of your choice as thanks.

# Contents

How to use this guide                                              6
Key maps                                                          7
Distance checklist                                                11

## Part One: Introduction                                         14

Pleasures of the South Downs Way • Downland wildlife • Geology •
History of the Downs • Practical advice • Cyclists • Horseriders

## Part Two: South Downs Way                                      30

  1  Eastbourne to Alfriston: footpath section                    32

  2  Eastbourne to Alfriston: bridleway                           46

  3  Alfriston to the A27 Crossing                                54

  4  A27 Crossing to Pyecombe                                     68

  5  Pyecombe to Upper Beeding                                    76

  6  Upper Beeding to Washington                                  86

  7  Washington to Amberley                                       96

  8  Amberley to Cocking                                          104

  9  Cocking to Buriton                                           116

 10  Buriton to Exton                                             124

 11  Exton to Winchester                                          136

## Part Three: Useful Information                                 145

Transport • Accommodation and Tourist Information Centres • Cyclists •
Walking and cycling holidays • Horseriders • Farriers • Horsebox parking
• Vets • Local facilities • Local organisations • Other useful addresses •
Guided walks • Bibliography • Ordnance Survey Maps

Circular walks appear on pages 42, 64 and 114

# How to use this guide

This guide to the 100-mile (160-kilometre) South Downs Way is in three parts:

• The introduction, with a historical background to the area and advice for walkers, horseriders and cyclists.

• The Way itself, split into eleven chapters, with maps opposite the description for each route section. The distances noted with each chapter represent the total length of the South Downs Way, including sections through towns and villages. This part of the guide also includes information on places of interest as well as a number of short walks which can be taken around parts of the path. Key sites are numbered both in the text and on the maps to make it easier to follow the route description.

• The last part includes useful information such as local transport, accommodation and organisations involved with the South Downs Way.

The maps have been prepared by the Ordnance Survey for this Trail Guide using 1:25 000 Explorer maps as a base. The line of the South Downs Way is shown in yellow, with the status of each section of the trail – footpath or bridleway, for example – shown in green underneath (see key on inside front cover). These rights-of-way markings also indicate the precise alignment of the South Downs Way, which you should try to follow. In some cases, the yellow line on these maps may show a route that is different from that shown on older maps; you are recommended to follow the yellow route in this guide, which will be the route that is waymarked with the distinctive acorn symbol 🔲 used for all National Trails. Any parts of the South Downs Way that may be difficult to follow on the ground are clearly highlighted in the route description, and important points to watch for are marked with letters in each chapter, both in the text and on the maps. *Some maps start on a right-hand page and continue on the left-hand page – black arrows (→) at the edge of the maps indicate the start point.*

Should there be a need to divert the South Downs Way from the route shown in this guide, for maintenance work or because the route has had to be changed, you are advised to follow any waymarks or signs along the path.

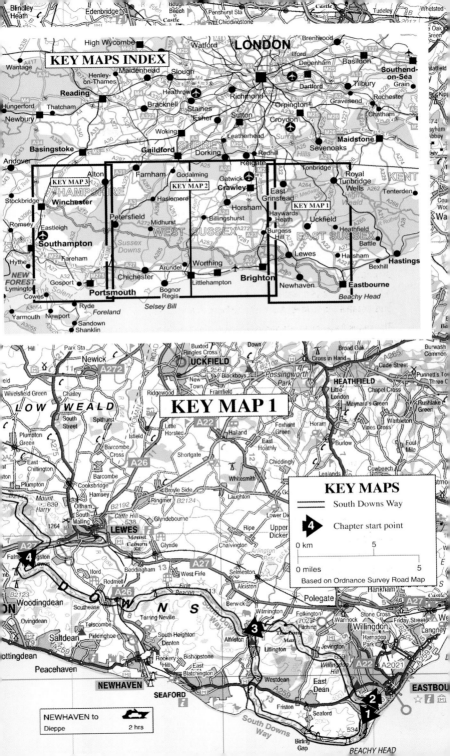

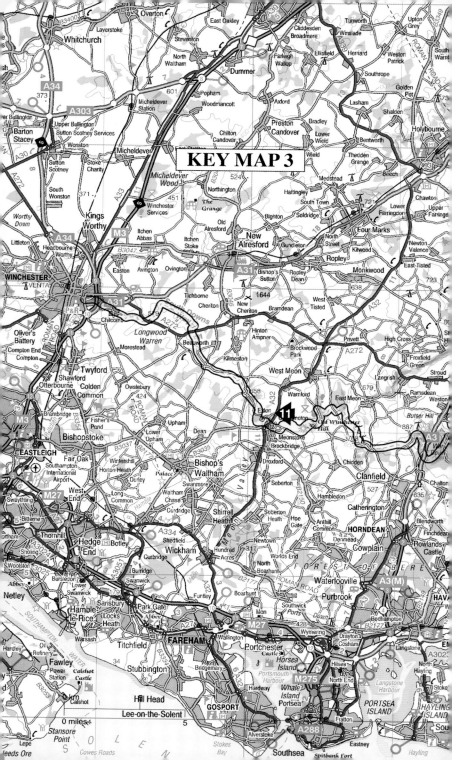

# KEY MAP 3

# Distance checklist

This list will assist you in calculating the distances between your proposed overnight accommodation and in checking your progress along the walk.

| location | approx. distance from previous location | |
|---|---|---|
| | miles | km |
| *footpath section* | | |
| Eastbourne | 0 | 0 |
| Birling Gap | 3.8 | 6.1 |
| Exceat | 3.7 | 6.0 |
| Westdean | 0.3 | 0.5 |
| Litlington | 1.5 | 2.4 |
| Alfriston | 1.3 | 2.1 |
| *bridleway* | | |
| Eastbourne | 0 | 0 |
| Jevington | 4.2 | 6.8 |
| Alfriston | 3.8 | 6.1 |
| Southease railway station | 7.0 | 11.3 |
| Southease | 0.6 | 1.0 |
|    Telscombe Youth Hostel (off route) | 1.7 | 2.7 |
| A27 Crossing | 6.2 | 10.0 |
|    Lewes railway station (off route) | 2.5 | 4.0 |
| Ditchling Beacon | 5.3 | 8.5 |
|    Ditchling (off route) | 1.3 | 2.1 |
| Clayton Windmills | 1.8 | 2.9 |
| Pyecombe | 1.3 | 2.1 |
| Devil's Dyke | 2.7 | 4.3 |
| Truleigh Hill Youth Hostel | 2.6 | 4.2 |
| A283 (water point) for Upper Beeding | 1.6 | 2.6 |
|    Upper Beeding (off route) | 0.8 | 1.3 |
|    Steyning (off route) | 2.0 | 3.2 |
| Chanctonbury Ring | 5.3 | 8.5 |
| A24 bus stop/car park | 1.5 | 2.4 |
| Washington | 0.6 | 1.0 |
| Chantry Post car park | 2.2 | 3.5 |
|    via Washington | 3.1 | 5.0 |
|    Arundel Youth Hostel (off route) | 5.0 | 8.0 |
| B2139 for Amberley railway station | 3.9 | 6.3 |
|    Arundel Youth Hostel (off route) (via North Stoke and river bank) | 4.0 | 6.4 |
|    Arundel (off route) (via river bank) | 4.6 | 7.4 |
| Toby's Stone (Bignor Hill) | 3.9 | 6.3 |
| Bignor Hill car park (Stane Street) | 0.6 | 1.0 |
| Littleton Farm (A285) | 2.1 | 3.4 |
| Tegleaze Post | 0.9 | 1.4 |

| | | |
|---|---|---|
| Graffham Post | 1.1 | 1.8 |
| Cocking Hill car park | 3.3 | 5.3 |
| Weald and Downland Museum (off route) | 2.8 | 4.5 |
| Cocking (off route) | 0.7 | 1.1 |
| Devil's Jumps Ancient Monument | 3.2 | 5.1 |
| Hookway (public house) (off route) | 0.7 | 1.1 |
| Harting Hill car park | 4.0 | 6.4 |
| South Harting (off route) | 0.7 | 1.1 |
| County boundary (Hampshire/West Sussex) | 2.0 | 3.2 |
| Queen Elizabeth Country Park | 1.9 | 3.1 |
| Buriton Church (off route) | 0.5 | 0.8 |
| Park Visitor Centre | 1.9 | 3.0 |
| Butser Hill | 0.8 | 1.3 |
| HMS *Mercury* (site of Sustainability Centre) | 2.5 | 4.0 |
| Old Winchester Hill (Nature Reserve) | 4.2 | 6.8 |
| Exton | 2.7 | 4.3 |
| Milbury's (public house) | 3.9 | 6.3 |
| Cheesefoot Head car park | 4.6 | 7.4 |
| Winchester | 3.5 | 5.6 |

# Trailblaze

At intervals along the whole route of the South Downs Way you will come across small white electronic boxes marked with the flaming logo of the Trailblaze system. This is an experimental approach to the management of the numbers of runners using the National Trail network. It allows individual runners to log their journey times automatically and thus aims to spread the load of this type of trail use. If the experiment is successful, then your peaceful walk or ride should not be spoilt by large groups of runners. Twenty per cent of the charges levied by the Trailblaze fees are passed to Natural England to aid with the cost of National Trail maintenance. For more information, go to www.trail-blaze.com

A Trailblaze log-in b
Saddlescombe (Chapte

*The Seven Sisters, East Sussex.*

# PART ONE
# Introduction

*The wide open spaces of the Downs seen from Windover Hill, looking west towards Firle Beacon.*

# Pleasures along the South Downs Way

In the 21st century why would anyone want to walk or ride 100 miles (160 km) along the South Downs Way between Eastbourne and Winchester?

There may be far easier methods of travel available, but to journey along this ancient route, away from the traffic, noise and dirt of the main roads, is an experience not to be missed. The pressures of modern urban life seem to put stresses on the human mind while failing adequately to exercise the body. To step back in time, and voyage by simple means along this historic ridgetop, is one of the best ways of reviving the spirit.

The sheer sense of space on top of the Downs is hard to describe. On clear days you can see so far, and from such a height, that it is almost like flying. In early morning or evening light, strong shadows give the rounded outlines of these hills a special texture. Whatever the time of year, there are so many sights to discover: Saxon and Norman churches, tumuli (the graves of settlers from over 3,000 years ago), medieval field systems where meagre crops were grown, and dew ponds from the days of the huge 18th- and 19th-century sheep flocks.

Seeing sheep still grazing the Downs and the butterflies feeding on the wild flowers gives the traveller a tremendous sense of continuity. High on top of the dry, streamless hills you can get closer to the mind of the shepherd, pedlar or pilgrim who journeyed on this path centuries ago.

The South Downs Way is a particularly attractive National Trail for the uninitiated. You can quickly achieve a feeling of quiet isolation, even solitude, while actually staying close to civilisation. The path is well used in summer, but as soon as you turn off the Way, into the heart of the Downs, there are opportunities to discover your own special places.

The underlying chalk geology makes this path one of the best for all-year-round journeys in Britain. The ground may be a little sticky in winter, but generally it is not a quagmire! It is easy to see why the Downs were chosen as ancient highways.

For the day or weekend traveller, the South Downs are ideally suited because of their accessibility. You can put a mountain bike on the train in London and, in just over an hour, get off at Glynde, Berwick, Lewes or other stations, in, or close to, this National Park.

The other main attraction of the South Downs – to the uninitiated or unfit – is that, overall, the walking, riding and cycling are easy! The paths are well-maintained, the stiles and gates are in good repair and clearly waymarked. In fact, the Downs have such a good path network that it is not difficult to take quite small children along with you. This is the ideal family area for exploring the countryside – at the eastern end you even have the sea!

Footprints of Sussex organises an annual group walk over the whole length of the route. For details see: www.south downsway.com. The South Downs Society produce a cloth badge for those who want to commemorate their completion of this wonderful journey (see page 155 for address).

# Downland wildlife

The combination of shallow, dry, chalk soils and low nutrient levels, due to constant grazing by sheep, has created a manmade habitat – effectively a grass desert. This 'desert' can now be seen only in remnants along the scarp slopes and sections of the Downs too steep for arable farming.

Surprisingly, this inhospitable habitat supports a huge variety of plants especially adapted to the environment. Where no fertilisers have been applied, up to 50 species can be found in each square metre. Sit on undisturbed chalk grassland in the summer and, among the sheep's fescue and upright brome grass, you will find flowering plants with strange names, such as salad burnet, squinancywort, round-headed rampion, scabious, and autumn lady's tresses. In spring you can still find thousands of cowslips, while later in the summer, attracted by food plants, over 20 species of butterfly, including silver-spotted skippers and adonis blues, can be seen. Insects other than butterflies are also common and close inspection of chalk grassland will reveal many types of snails, moths and grasshoppers. Useful indicators of undisturbed, herb-rich grassland are the hills of the yellow meadow ant. These low grassy lumps, about a foot (30 cm) high, show that the ground has not been ploughed for many years.

The observant traveller can find early purple and common spotted orchids, and with more care you might see burnt, fragrant, pyramidal, frog, musk, bee and green-winged varieties.

Almost certainly you will see rooks nesting in the ash and beech woodland or feeding on the corn stubble, jackdaws and seagulls at Beachy Head, skylarks everywhere, and kestrels hovering above looking for a juicy beetle. Pheasant and partridge are often disturbed, and in the valleys there are herons fishing in the drainage ditches and cormorants on the rivers.

Fortunately, in 1987 much of the Downs were declared an Environmentally Sensitive Area and farmers have been encouraged by grant aid to move back to traditional grazing with no fertilisers or pesticides.

# Geology

Most people think of the Downs as a smooth, almost treeless, landscape. The rocks that form the Downs and Weald are made from sediments laid down in both freshwater lakes and seas many millions of years ago, then raised by earth movements and bent into a huge dome about 125 miles (200 km) long and 50 miles (80 km) wide. Being soft, it began to be eroded by the rain and wind as soon as it was raised above the sea. This natural erosion is still going on today.

The top layer of the sedimentary sandwich was chalk, with some younger deposits, made up of the remains of shells of creatures that lived in the warm Cretaceous seas, during a period so long that sediments hundreds of yards thick were deposited. Their scale can best be seen where the modern sea has sliced through the chalk along the cliffs between Beachy Head and Cuckmere Haven. After winter storms have caused cliff-falls it is possible to find among the rocks fossilised shells of animals that lived 75 million years ago. The chalk is not only being eroded where the sea meets it today, but also where the top is

Grants, such as Environmental Stewardship, encourage farmers to maintain wildlife strips, often filled with arable wild flowers.

exposed to the elements. Over time the dome has worn away, and all that remains of the chalk deposits are the North and South Downs.

How did the rivers cut through the Downs? Why are there valleys without streams or rivers in them? Where do all the flints come from?

The great dome was formed very slowly and the Cuckmere, Ouse, Adur and Arun Rivers had time to cut their way through the soft chalk. The valleys without streams, such as Devil's Dyke, were

clearly cut by water, either in a much wetter climate, which would have led to a higher water table, or during the Ice Ages, when permafrost would have made the chalk temporarily impervious.

Today the chalk is filled with rainwater like a huge sponge, and towns such as Eastbourne and Brighton derive much of their drinking water from these underground sources. However, in the wetter parts of the year, streams do flow in some of the dry valleys, and the 'Winterbourne', which rises near The Newmarket Inn and flows through

Lewes to the River Ouse, is a classic example.

Flint, which is the only hard and brittle rock to be found on the Downs, is a remarkable material – basically silica that was precipitated by chemical processes and replaced the chalk (calcium carbonate) around it. As the chalk eroded, the lumps of hard flint were left behind. It was probably once liquid, as it forms in organic shapes and has been known to fill the voids left by dead sea creatures to form 'flint' fossils. When you visit the cliffs it is possible to see clear seams of flints laid down as narrow bands in the chalk. Shortly after ploughing, some of the fields of the Downs have the appearance of a stony wasteland, as flints rise to the surface.

Flints may seem simply to be a hard surfacing to the downland trackways, but their importance in terms of human development should not be underestimated. Early people found that they could use the razor-sharp edges of flaked flint as a cutting tool and over many thousands of years they refined their techniques until quite sophisticated knives, arrowheads and axes could be made. Such was the importance of this mineral that it led to the establishment of specialised industrial workings, such as the flint mines on Windover Hill, and the early development of trade over a wide area. It was perhaps the presence of flint on the Downs that led to this area being the focus of early British civilisation. The later use of flint with iron to 'strike a light', and thus make fire-lighting relatively simple, combined with the use of the sparks from flint and iron in early flint-lock guns, confirmed the position of this odd, little understood mineral as one of the great keys to European development.

With no hard rock present on the chalk Downs, flint has also been the only naturally occurring building material, and in its various forms is very much part of the rural landscape.

# History of the Downs

Between 500,000 and 12,000 years ago (the Old Stone Age), small numbers of nomadic people occasionally wandered the Downs and coastal fringe, hunting deer, wild boar, birds and fish. It was pretty bleak then and the climate shifted back and forth between long periods of freezing cold, during the Ice Ages, and temperate conditions. The ice never spread south far enough to cover the Downs, but its influence made the vegetation tundra-like. When the ice finally melted 10,000 years ago, forests developed and the still-nomadic population of the Middle Stone Age grew.

The land bridge that had linked Britain to the Continent was finally breached by the rising sea.

*Rackham Banks Iron Age earthworks, near Amberley, West Sussex.*

Then, roughly 5,000 years ago, the New Stone Age (Neolithic) people crossed the narrow sea and settled the Downs. They brought with them a new, more sophisticated culture, which included semi-nomadic agriculture, pottery, flint mining and trade. This fundamental shift from simple hunters and gatherers to a tribal people who kept domestic animals and cleared the trees to grow crops began changing the Downs from forested hills to the open rolling landscape we see today.

You will pass many landscape features that date from Neolithic times (around 3000 BC). There are large enclosures at Combe Hill (above Jevington) and Barkhale (on Bignor Hill). Archaeological excavations suggest that these were put to a variety of uses, including settlements, meeting places, stock-gathering grounds and ceremonial events. Another remarkable group of Neolithic features occasionally to be found along the Way are long barrows. These earth mounds, up to 200 feet (60 metres) long and sited on dominant hills, were the communal graves of extended families or clan groups.

Around 2500 BC, communal graves gave way to single burials in the form of round barrows, marked on the maps as 'tumuli'. There are many hundreds of these low, circular mounds on the high ground along the South Downs Way. Between 2000 BC, when the first tumuli were constructed, and 1000 BC, a more advanced Bronze Age civilisation developed, based on settled agriculture with farmsteads of round buildings surrounded by a rectangular field. Such a settlement of 13 round huts within a protective fence was established on Itford Hill around 1000 BC and there was a similar settlement at Plumpton Plain.

This high, dry route along the top of the Downs must have been an important part of the Bronze Age trading network that brought jet from Yorkshire, gold from Ireland and amber from Scandinavia. Over a dozen hoards of bronze tools and weapons have been found on the Sussex Downs and they confirm the Way as a significant trade route.

The Bronze Age economy was based on mixed farming and there are many landscape features of this period along the route. The 'cross dykes' were probably farm boundaries, and the large enclosures that are visible may have been stock pens of some kind, such as those at Butser Hill and Belle Tout.

Around 650 BC iron began to be used, and as Celtic settlers from the Continent brought more of the new metal with them, a further cultural and technological change took place. Nevertheless, the Iron Age people lived very similar lives to those of the Bronze Age, with round houses and settled agriculture, but the population grew and some sort of crop rotation and fertilisation of the arable land evolved. More than 60 Iron Age farmsteads are known in Sussex and the increasing population, equipped with sharp iron tools, probably led to more of the remaining chalk woodland being cleared for agriculture or felled for fuel.

The most obvious Iron Age monuments are the camps and hill forts built around 300–200 BC. It is now believed that these forts were the product of tribal rivalry. They are all on high, defensive positions and consisted of a circular bank and ditches. Some are relatively small and simple, like that at Chanctonbury, but there are more elaborate forts at Devil's Dyke, Old Winchester Hill and Cissbury Ring.

The field systems created by the Iron Age farmers were a common downland sight until modern methods led to their being ploughed out. The best remaining examples to be seen from the Way are on the flanks of Combe Hill, near Jevington, and at Balmer Down, near Brighton. These small rectangular fields (usually less than 2 acres or 1 hectare) are still noticeable, because they were farmed for so long that they effectively formed blocks of terraces with clear lynchets (banks) up to 10 feet (3 metres) high.

Sussex and the downland area were also very important to the Romans. This area was a strategic bridgehead for the conquest of the rest of Britain and it was commercially vital for iron from the Weald and corn and meat from the Downs. There are still remains of Roman roads running from Chichester and Lewes to London; Roman villas, such as that at Bignor, and country houses and farmsteads have been found all along the scarp foot.

Generally, little changed for the local downland people, but during this settled period they started to establish significant hamlets and villages for the first time.

Sussex was one of the first parts of Roman Britain to be conquered and colonised by the Saxons. *The Anglo-Saxon Chronicle* tells us that a small band of Saxons came by ship and landed somewhere between Beachy Head and Selsey Bill around AD 477. But instead of developing the high Downs, which had already been farmed for over 2,000 years, they opted for the better soils of the downland valleys and scarp foot.

Each long, narrow parish had land for pigs and cattle in the clay Weald –

arable land at the scarp foot and sheep grazing on the Downs. Walking along the South Downs Way you can see at a glance whole parishes that formed the basis of the early Anglo-Saxon settlement of southern Sussex.

Tracks, or 'droveways', developed between the villages at the foot of the Downs and the Wealden pastures. If you look at the Ordnance Survey maps these parallel, north–south roads are quite clear and some pass distinctly through gaps in the Downs or tracks cut across the scarp, as at Chanctonbury, Storrington, Steyning and Rackham Bank.

Between the 8th and 9th centuries there was a reorganisation of this scattered peasant population into nucleated villages, so that they could communally farm the land more effectively. Large areas of lighter soils around the village sites would have been cleared, and these islands of cultivation within woodland at the scarp foot would have been visible from the South Downs Way. However, the High Weald would still have been largely forest, even at the time of the Norman Conquest in 1066.

The Sussex Saxons rejected Christianity for longer than people in other parts of England, but once they had accepted it they quickly built churches – unpretentious structures made of local materials. The Normans continued this Christian tradition and by 1086 a parish church was an integral part of every Sussex village.

From the Norman invasion until the Black Death of 1348 was a period of population expansion. The existing communities grew and new market towns and seaports were established. The Church owned huge estates and the

large barns at Alciston, Wilmington and Bishopstone attest to its efficient farming methods. It was in this period that the basic system of downland sheep combined with scarp-foot corn was developed. Each day the shepherd brought his flock off the hill tops and penned them on the stubble and fallow of the arable soil at the base of the Downs. This system of using sheep as a 'mobile dunging machine' created a profitable and sustainable farming system. The wool was worked into cloth by artisans in the Weald or traded across the Channel with Flanders.

The plague of the 14th century severely reduced the population. Some villages, such as Exceat, became completely deserted and many others, such as Botolphs and Coombes, shrank in size. The downland continued to be farmed but the large peasant population it once supported declined, and by the end of the 17th century one single sheep 'ranch' commonly occupied a whole parish.

Another influence on the downland landscape was the 17th-and 18th-century growth of chalk quarrying, to lime the acid Wealden land and to provide building mortar. This was combined with a brief period of canal building and improved river navigation on the Arun and Ouse, to move the chalk from the downland quarries to the Weald.

Many isolated flint 'manure' barns were built between 1780 and 1840 to house the oxen used for ploughing and to hold the increased corn harvest of this period.

The growth of the resorts from little more than fishing towns was due to turnpike road improvements and to sea-bathing becoming fashionable. Surprisingly, in the 18th century the open nature of the downland landscape was no longer popular and considerable sums were spent on landscaping, as at Stanmer Park. The resorts were given huge impetus by the Napoleonic Wars – not only was it impossible to visit the Continent, but also troops were stationed along the coast, providing a richer social life in the seaside towns. This, combined with royal patronage and the coming of the railway, led to much of the coastal fringe of the Downs being covered in housing. Places such as Brighton, Hove and Worthing outstripped the county towns in size. Fortunately, this process, combined with the lack of 19th-century industrial development, stopped the growth of the older towns and has left us with such gems as Lewes, Chichester and Arundel.

By the end of the 19th century, cheap food from Australia and the prairies of North America had made downland farming unprofitable. Much of the arable land reverted to sheep grazing or scrub and some farmers began to sell off their land to property developers.

Between 1900 and 1945 residential development spread on to some of the remaining parts of the downland coastline. Eventually the despoliation was so great that individuals, charities and local authorities bought the land between Eastbourne and Seaford in order to

protect it. The Town and Country Planning Act 1947 brought speculative house building under control. Since then, the route you follow between Beachy Head and Winchester has been further protected in various ways. The Downs have finally been designated as a National Park and there are a number of national and local nature reserves. Much of the scarp is a Site of Special Scientific Interest and public access land. Many of the buildings have been listed and the best remaining undamaged archaeological features are Scheduled Ancient Monuments.

Despite all these conservation measures, the destruction of the old downland by 'high tech' agriculture has happened on a scale, and at a speed, never before contemplated. Nevertheless, today's traveller will still find these rolling hills, with their mixture of corn, woods and grassland, immensely beautiful.

# Practical advice

The most important basic rule to follow is 'keep it light'. The temptation to take too much equipment on a long journey, or even a day trip, should be strongly resisted. In winter the winds can be biting, so a warm waterproof hat or hood is essential – ideally it should shelter the ears! Some form of lightweight, windproof, wet-weather gear is also necessary, preferably something that breathes. It is also important to be warm; long underwear, wool trousers and jumpers help. If your top clothes have front zips or buttons they can be opened if you get too hot. In summer some form of comfortable shade is vital. Remember to have long shirt sleeves, so that they can be rolled down to protect arms from sunburn.

Plan your route, especially if travelling for several days. Each section of this guide covers a comfortable day's walking in winter light. Cyclists and horseriders can obviously cover greater distances. Get all the extra maps you require if you intend to go off the edge of those in this guide. Youth hostels can be full all year round, so try to book in advance. See the Useful Information section at the back of this book for help in finding bed and breakfast accommodation. There are also a number of campsites along the Way (though few as yet in the Hampshire section). If asked, most farmers will give permission to camp.

A compass is very useful – it looks complicated but at least it will tell you where north is. If you get completely lost in thick mist or fog on the Way (which is unlikely), walk any path northwards and you are sure to hit a road.

Carry some liquid refreshment – a flask of hot tea in winter or some water in summer – and a snack. Water points are marked in the guide but the distance between them can be considerable. Your basic minimal equipment should include: this guide book; a compass to help you follow the directions in this guide; a small first-aid kit (plasters for blisters and crêpe bandage for strains); a whistle, just in case you need to give the recognised distress signal of 6 blasts – 3 in reply; a small torch with new batteries – there is nothing worse than flat batteries if you are stuck at night; a small day pack or saddlebags for carrying all this equipment (try to keep it below 22 lb/10 kg); lightweight wet-weather clothing – especially in the winter; boots or strong shoes you know are comfortable (do not try to break in a pair of new boots by walking the whole

South Downs Way – you are guaranteed to get blisters!); a pair of dry socks; a watch, to ensure correct bus and train connections; refreshments; emergency loo paper; a hat; a mobile phone plus charger – vital, as so many phone boxes have been disconnected recently.

You may also wish to take: a map case for wet weather; suntan lotion in summer; gloves; field guides; binoculars (lightweight); camera; tent and sleeping bag (as lightweight as possible) if camping; sunglasses – the glare from bare chalk or snow can be quite strong; penknife; any special medication.

It is sensible to eat a substantial breakfast before setting out, as you cannot be sure of arriving at a pub or café exactly at lunchtime. Nowadays most pubs serve food and one of the joys of a day's journey on the Downs is to drop down off the top to a scarp-foot or valley-floor village and eat a good meal before setting off for the afternoon. Some pubs also have family rooms, offer B&B for users of the Way, and sometimes serve evening meals.

The larger towns all have excellent facilities. Eastbourne, Brighton and Winchester are within easy reach of the Downs and offer a variety of shopping, as well as specialist shops for cyclists and riders. The county town of Lewes lies close to the Way. It, and also Arundel, has quite a reasonable range of shops, and hotels and bed and breakfast accommodation. Many smaller villages have a general store and post office combined.

Wednesday is often half-day closing. In the larger towns many shops stay open but in the smaller centres most are closed in the afternoon.

# Cyclists

Obviously a good quality, all-terrain bike with front suspension and 21 gears or more is best, but in summer it is possible to cycle along the Way on an ordinary bike with tough tyres. This does involve a lot of pushing up hills, and really 12 gears is the minimum requirement.

The cyclist needs to take certain basic extra equipment – the following is advised: a lightweight safety helmet (if you come off and hit your head on a flint, it could be rather nasty!); a good basic tool kit, including puncture repair, spare brake pads, at least one spare inner tube and oil for lubricating the chain; a handlebar map holder can save a lot of fiddling about, as can waterbottles fixed to the bike; panniers well secured to the bike rather than a day sack; working lights and a bell.

Choose the right clothing for the trip. In summer, wear something that is easy to open or put on and take off. Shorts are more comfortable than long trousers in summer, but not necessarily on the tougher narrow sections, where nettles can be a problem.

Hiking boots are heavy and trainers offer no ankle support on the flinty surfaces when pushing a bike uphill. Special mountain-biking boots are best, but some sort of lightweight rambling boot would be a reasonable compromise. As with walking, keep gear to a minimum.

A few helpful tips: if you have your tyres pumped up too hard, the ride is uncomfortable, but if they are too soft, the flints cut the side walls; if you get a puncture from a thorn and do not realise that this has happened, when you put the repaired tube back in the tyre it will immediately puncture again; if cycling during the winter, watch out for your tyre pump getting clogged up with mud. See pages 146–8 for shops specialising in spare parts for bikes and The Mountain Bike Code.

*Lewes, with its Norman priory and castle.*

# Horseriders

Wear footwear that you know is comfortable. Rubber boots tend to make your feet sweat and are cold in winter. A long, wet-weather riding coat or cape with hood is needed for bad weather and a hard hat that fits well is essential. A peak on your hat will offer some additional shade in summer.

Good, new shoes on a fit horse are, of course, basic, and all your tack should be in tip-top condition. Road studs (not the screw-in type, to avoid jarring the horse) might be helpful in icy conditions. Carry some feed (nuts are less bulky than oats). And a particularly useful item is a rope halter or head halter to tie up your horse while you have your own meals.

There is a good deal of thorn and blackthorn along sections of the Way, so strong riding trousers are needed and leather chaps can protect your legs even more. Shoes are better than boots if you have to walk any distance, and if you wear short boots or riding shoes, leather gaiters will help.

Saddles for long-distance riding have a wider seat than standard; some people prefer western-style kit for comfort. It is possible to get sheepskin covers that slip over your saddle and can significantly reduce long-distance soreness. Rubbing reins can be abrasive, so gloves are useful, not only for warmth but also for offering some protection.

Saddlebags are the best way to carry your gear and some saddle cloths have pockets that are ideal for your guide and other items.

A small grooming kit, of a dandy brush and hoof pick, and a first-aid kit for horses are essential. Your horse may be cut by flints above the fetlocks while crossing ploughed fields, so take antibiotic powder in a puffer and bandages.

You can ride the Eastbourne to Buriton section of the Way in a weekend on a fit horse. The extension to Winchester will add a day. Naturally, the journey can be taken at a more leisurely pace and sometimes stony ground makes walking necessary.

Get off once an hour for about five minutes to rest both yourself and the horse. When you stop, loosen the girth and resettle the saddle. This lets the blood in the horse's back recirculate. After long-distance riding it is vital to take proper care of your horse. To avoid serious swelling do not remove the saddle straight away: leave it for five to ten minutes to allow the blood to return slowly, rather than in a rush. After removing, slap the horse's back where the saddle was; this will help the blood to start circulating .

To help your horse relax and dry off at the end of the day, finish your journey at a walk. Let the girth out a single hole shortly before you stop. Initially it is important to let your horse drink no more than half a bucket of water, in order to avoid colic. If your horse is tired, keep it dry and warm, especially if you have had to sponge it down. At night remember to visit your horse regularly to make sure it has not started to sweat.

*Looking down into the valley of the Arun from the South Downs Way.*

## PART TWO
# South Downs Way

# Eastbourne to Alfriston

**Footpath section:** *via Birling Gap and Litlington*

*10½ miles (16.9 km)*

**Ascent** 2,520 feet (770 metres)
**Descent** 2,670 feet (815 metres)
**Highest point** Beachy Head: 530 feet (160 metres)
**Lowest point** River Cuckmere: 3 feet (1 metre)

The South Downs Way footpath starts at the western end of Eastbourne promenade. It is possible to get buses to the start, but if you want to walk, follow the signposts from the station to the South Downs Way up Grove Road, past the Town Hall and through the Meads district (shops). Alternatively, go south-east to the sea front, so you can see the pier and Martello tower as you head westwards along the promenade.

The Way begins next to a small kiosk **A**, shuttered in late winter, but where, for most of the year, you can buy refreshments. It takes about half an hour of gentle walking from the railway station to reach this point.

The path rises steeply as a thin chalky line in a landscape of downland and scattered scrub. To the south lies the Channel, stretching out to the horizon. On a clear day, looking east, you can see as far as Hastings, the Fairlight Cliffs, perhaps even Dungeness. The windswept thorns show what a bleak spot this can be.

About 220 yards (200 metres) from the kiosk, after climbing a flight of concrete steps, you come to a broad mown area. Carry on another 30 yards to a waymark post at a junction of paths. Take the

southernmost of two forks and head into the scrub along a broad mown strip. As you rise, the wind can pick up. The scrub, with its stunted thorn, ash and sycamore, offers some shelter, but in summer this can be a hot, steep climb, though there are wild raspberries and blackberries which give an excuse for the occasional pause as well as providing nourishment to help you along!

Go south-westwards, with fire rides creating a maze of paths. The ground falls steeply away to the south into Whitebread Hole, a scrub-filled combe. This is a safe haven for birds migrating across the Channel. In winter there are fine tufts of old man's beard strung among the branches and magpies flit among the trees. There is an abundance of purple rosebay willowherb, which, in season, sends great drifts of white seed blowing across the Downs.

As you reach the edge of the scrub you can see cars driving along the Beachy Head road. Here you pass another waymark post and walk a short distance on open grassland in a south-easterly direction. Down below lie the playing fields on the floor of Whitebread Hole.

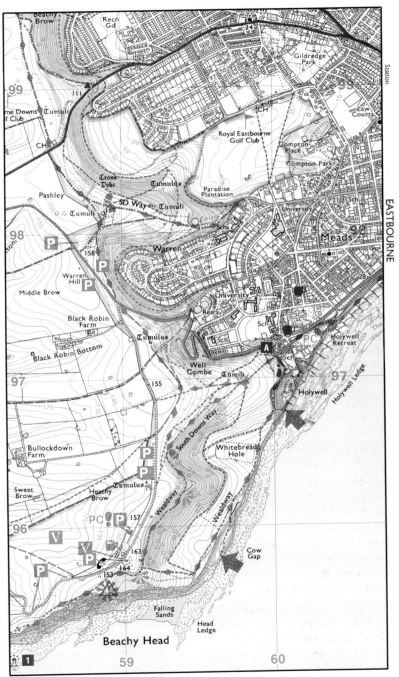

Contours are given in metres
The vertical interval is 5m

*Belle Tout ceased functioning as a lighthouse in 1901 and is now a private house.*

About 200 yards (180 metres) ahead, a fingerpost directs you into the scrub again along a narrow, winding path that follows the contours. Occasionally the thorn thins out and the views down to the sea are superb. Below you may see sheep grazing the clifftop downland. There is a lot of poisonous climbing white bryony and, in the more open areas, chalk downland flowers. After

550 yards (500 metres) you come to a stretch of crumbling tarmac and cross the lighter-coloured 'Peace Path' twice (commemorating United Nations Peace Year). From here, the trail dips round the head of a cut-off dry valley. To the north is the main car park with nearby public toilet and Beachy Head Inn (rebuilt after a disastrous fire) with an adjoining visitor centre.

At Beachy Head you occasionally see hang-gliders. To the west you can make out Belle Tout, which was the lighthouse for this stretch of coast between 1834 and 1901. The octagonal brick shelter on the cliff top is the base of a 19th-century signalling station. From here messages were sent to the London offices of Lloyd's Insurance brokers confirming the safe arrival of ships and cargoes.

As you pass, walk south-westwards towards the cliff edge. If you don't suffer from vertigo, look down 530 feet (160 metres) to the Beachy Head lighthouse **1**. In misty weather the noise of the foghorn gives the whole area an eerie atmosphere. The lighthouse was built in 1902 by steam-winching huge stone blocks from the top of the cliffs down to the sea. This wonderful landmark was last repainted by Trinity House in 2001 and sports bright 'candy stripes'.

From this viewpoint the South Downs Way follows the cliff line westwards to Birling Gap. The sea can be stained a milky white by the eroding chalk and,

when the tide is out, you can see the flat, wave-cut platform. This is one of the only undeveloped stretches of coast left in south-east England and is defined as a Heritage Coast by Natural England.

To the north lies Hodcombe Farm, a private house surrounded by stunted trees, and a favourite bird-ringing station for ornithologists. At Shooters' Bottom there are three yellow concrete markers in the turf. These indicators were used to measure rates of cliff erosion from aerial photographs.

Belle Tout **2** is now a private residence, but as part of the filming for a television series its canopy was replaced, so it still retains a maritime character. Eventually, despite having been moved away from the cliff edge, this redundant lighthouse will fall into the sea, but for now it remains a precarious landmark.

From here you get tremendous views of the Seven Sisters cliffs. Head west on a broad, short turf track through low gorse towards the site of an old coastguard lookout and Bronze Age fort.

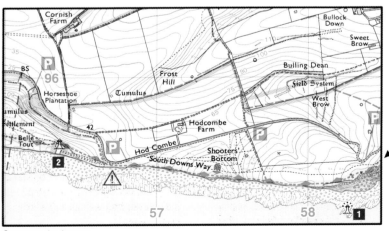

Contours are given in metres
The vertical interval is 5m

A short oak post marks where the coastguard tower stood and the area was known as Lookout Hill. In the Bronze Age the cliffs would have been at least 1¼ miles (2 km) further out to sea. Down to the west is Birling Gap with its café, pub, B&B, information centre, toilets, telephone, postbox and water point.

Rather surprisingly, the Way turns north about 55 yards (50 metres) past the short oak post and heads downhill to the main road. Turn south for 100 yards along the verge to reach Birling Gap itself. The National Trust acquired the Gap under its Enterprise Neptune scheme (set up to protect as much as possible of the most beautiful stretches of coastline in England and Wales) and has erected a viewing platform to help you see the Seven Sisters cliffs safely. There are also steps from this platform down to the beach.

From Birling Gap, the Way heads west again up a flinty track, past the new

toilets which look like a tarred fisherman's cottage. At the top, turn north where there is a waymark directing you for approximately 50 yards and then, at the next signpost, turn west again through a hunt gate.

Ahead is a kissing-gate leading on to Crowlink, one of the largest of the National Trust properties in East Sussex. Here you start walking the 'ups and downs' of the Seven Sisters. In the distance you can spot the brown clayey cap on the cliffs at Seaford Head Nature Reserve. Please respect the measures to control erosion on this section of the Way, and avoid rabbit holes!

Going up the western slope of Michel Dean you come to a concrete obelisk **3** commemorating the gift of this land to the National Trust by W. A. Robertson in memory of his two brothers, who were killed on the Somme during the First World War; a wonderful way to remember the brave dead.

At Flagstaff Brow there is another monument made from a sarsen stone. This sandstone boulder was stranded on top of the chalk 50 million years ago when the rocks above were eroded. On it is a plaque commemorating a further gift, which allowed the Society of Sussex Downsmen to purchase the Crowlink Valley in 1926. Below the cliff, at Flagstaff Bottom, there is a raised area of the wave-cut platform marked on the map as Flagstaff Point. When the tide is out you realise why so many ships foundered along this coastline. (At low tide you can visit the wreck of the *Coonata*.)

Gap Bottom **4** was another low point favoured by smugglers. You can just see the square outline of some now-demolished coastguard cottages.

*The Seven Sisters cliffs, looking west from the wave-cut platform at Birling Gap.*

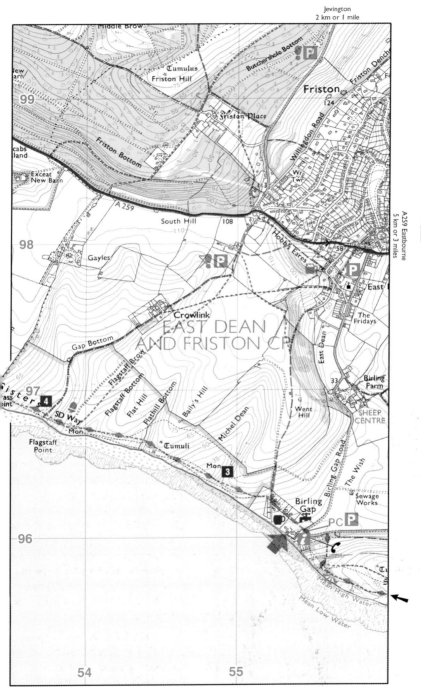

Contours are given in metres
The vertical interval is 5m

*The River Cuckmere meanders through its valley.*

The fence on the skyline at Brass Point marks the eastern boundary of Seven Sisters Country Park. Looking west from Rough Brow you can see the groynes of Cuckmere Haven and the cottages at Short Cliff. At Haven Brow the views over the Cuckmere Estuary are stunning. This is the only unspoilt estuary in the south-east and is really magnificent.

At a fingerpost the Way curves north above the steepest section of Haven Brow and runs diagonally across the slope above an area of scrub. Below, you can just see the remains of pill boxes that defended the Cuckmere Valley during the Second World War. The Country Park has been grazed by sheep and cattle with no fertiliser or herbicide application for almost 40 years. The artificial lagoon behind the raised shingle bank of the beach is a good site for waders, such as dunlin, ringed plover and redshank.

Pass through a hunt gate and, after two fingerposts and another two-way hunt gate, a little way up the valley, you meet a concrete farm road. This is the quickest route to Foxhole, where the Country Park campsite and camping barn lie. The Way now rises above the cut-off meanders **5** where the river was straightened and canalised in the 19th century.

The sheltered waters of the meanders attract dabchicks, tufted ducks and a large number of Canada geese in winter, and are popular with solitary herons and cormorants in summer. Go north-east via a kissing-gate towards the site of Exceat Church with the route occasionally marked by acorns on low waymark posts. From a kissing-gate near the top of Exceat Hill turn north to a marker stone at the site of the church that once served the now lost village of Exceat. Eastwards you can see the roof of New Barn and Friston Forest on the skyline. From the church site go downhill north-eastwards towards Exceat Farm with the cut-off meanders of the River Cuckmere below on the valley floor. The Environment Agency has been promoting a visionary conservation scheme to re-establish the cut-off meanders as the course of the Cuckmere and the flood plain as salt marsh.

Cross the road at the bus stop by the Country Park entrance, between a cycle-hire centre and a cottage, to a kissing-gate and a Trailblaze box. The nearby visitor centre has an exhibition on local wildlife and history, a gift shop and toilets. The excellent Exceat Farmhouse restaurant also has B&B facilities.

The Way heads almost north-east up the hill in the direction of Friston Forest and at the top goes through a hunt gate and over a notch in a flint wall **B**. Turn round at this point to look back at the local geology and the formation of the cut-off meanders **5**. From the waymark post, just beyond the flint stile, the path descends more than 200 steps through an archway of trees to Westdean village.

At the bottom, go past a Forestry Commission noticeboard, fingerpost and the village pond. After 100 yards travelling north-east on the metalled road there is a South Downs Way concrete plinth and an acorn attached to the telegraph pole signposting the Way ahead. (A brief diversion here will take you to the village church **6**.) Head for a gap next to a gate up a dirt track, leading into the Forestry Commission land, where there are a number of

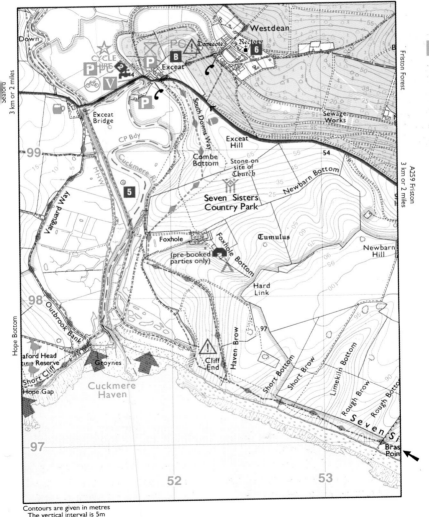

Contours are given in metres
The vertical interval is 5m

*Alfriston Clergy House. Originally built in 1350, this was the National Trust's first property, acquired in 1896 for £10.*

waymark posts indicating the route. The aim of planting this forest was to protect locally important underground water supplies from pollution, but for the walker it is the autumn colours, winter shelter or summer shade that make it attractive. The path curves gently to the north past a waymark post by the edge of the forest, between two fence strainers and down steps to the rear of Charleston Manor.

Take care descending as there are quite a lot of tree roots. At the foot of the steps a waymark directs you along a level, beech-lined track, not quite on the definitive route. After 100 yards turn due north over a stile beneath a cherry-plum tree. The Way now climbs alongside arable fields and a hedge. From the top of this small hill the great arc of the Cuckmere lies to the west, below High and Over and the White Horse **7**. To the north-east, Windover Hill dominates the landscape, with views up the valley to the Weald and a distant spire, which is Berwick Church.

Just before descending into Litlington past a double stile **C**, Alfriston is visible ahead on the west side of the river. You can see flint and tile cottages in the village below

as you descend through two kissing-gates. From here go west to the road and then north just past The Plough and Harrow **8**, where you turn west down a narrow pathway which leads down to a small bridge over the Cuckmere. If you wish, you can cross the river to Frog Firle Youth Hostel. (Litlington Tea Gardens just to the north of The Plough and Harrow are recommended for their refreshments and almost timeless atmosphere.)

Just before the bridge the Way turns north to meet the river floodbank. Watch out here for the occasional blue flash of a kingfisher and listen to the rustle of the dried phragmites reeds swaying in the wind. After passing through a kissing-gate follow the riverbank to Alfriston. It is worth looking at the wildlife of the drainage ditches alongside – dragonflies, damselflies and swans are common here. Where these ditches exit into the river you may see a metal flap which stops tidal saltwater flooding back into the grassy marshes. The path winds past the thatched Clergy House (the first property purchased by the National Trust) and the parish church of Alfriston to a white bridge where it joins the bridleway route.

For the rest of the route in East Sussex the waymarks are blue to denote its bridleway status. Once on the west bank, the bridleway turns north again and past a sign saying 'Horses'.

After approximately 50 yards you proceed west up River Lane towards Alfriston's square. To reach the car park and public toilets follow the signpost straight ahead through a farmyard.

The Way turns south briefly, down the High Street, and then west again between Steamer Trading and The Star Inn. Alfriston Youth Hostel is at Frog Firle, half a mile (1 km) south. You can reach it by a roadside footway or down the river-bank footpath.

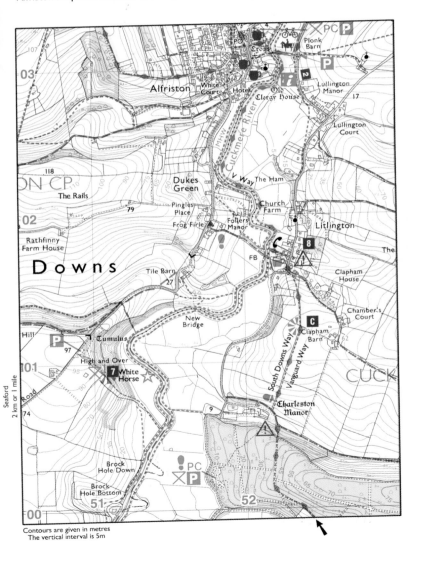

Contours are given in metres
The vertical interval is 5m

# A circular walk at Beachy Head

*8 miles (12.9 km)*

The area between Beachy Head and Birling Gap is part of a Voluntary Marine Conservation Area, and is one of the most beautiful unspoilt environments in the Downs – a true wilderness and particularly spectacular on spring low tides when the maximum area of the chalk wave-cut platform is exposed to view.

This circular walk is made up of two loops, one between Eastbourne and Beachy Head (3 miles/4.8 km), the other near Birling Gap (2 miles/3.1 km), linked by the South Downs Way itself. You can start this walk at either end and do as much or as little as you like.

Assuming that you start from Eastbourne, head in a southerly direction past Whitebread Hole, towards Cow Gap, where there is access to the

beach. As there is a risk of rock falls and rising tides, just take a quick look, then return up the steps and rejoin the circular walk. From here, continue parallel to the sea until the path turns right and heads westwards to meet the South Downs Way.

If you intend to walk only the short loop, turn right and head back (1¼ miles/2 km) into Eastbourne along the National Trail; otherwise, at the path junction turn left along the cliff tops towards Birling Gap. This link section (1½ miles/2.6 km) takes you past the Lloyd's lookout and Beachy Head lighthouse **1**, then downhill to meet the road. This is the point at which you start the second loop.

Continue westwards along the coast, past the disused lighthouse of Belle Tout **2**, until you reach a short oak post. Just past this, turn right and walk inland towards the road. When you are on the road, you can turn left and walk into Birling Gap, where there are refreshments, or continue by turning

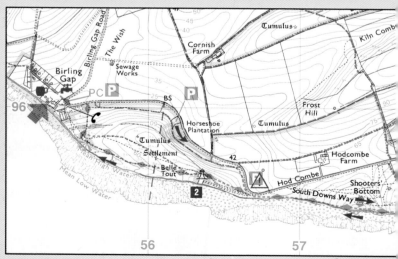

right along the road for a few yards, then taking the next turn on to a bridleway. This runs parallel with the road, passing Horseshoe Plantation until it once again joins the road, which you follow south back to the start of this loop and the South Downs Way.

To return to Eastbourne, follow the link, now in an easterly direction, past Shooters Bottom, to rejoin the first loop at the path junction. Keep on the National Trail, heading inland and looking down over your outward route, until you arrive back at the start of the circular walk.

*One of the many chalk rock pools that can be found along the Heritage Coast.*

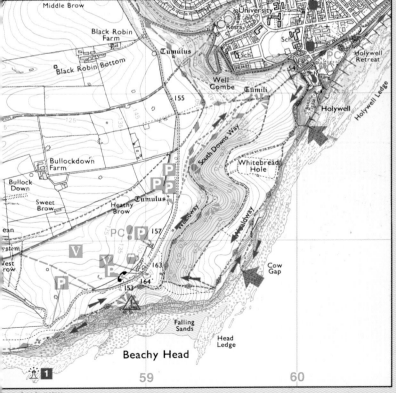

are given in metres
tical interval is 5m

The Battle of Beachy Head, 30 June 1690, *by Nicolas Ozanne (artist) and François Jacques Dequevauviller (engraver).*

*Beachy Head, seen from Belle Tout on the South Downs Way.*

# The Battle of Beachy Head

The Channel has seen many naval battles but in 1690, off Beachy Head, the Earl of Torrington may have invented the concept of deterrence. Commanding a combined English and Dutch fleet against the French — who believed they were supporting a Jacobite uprising — Torrington faced defeat and withdrew to the mouth of the Thames. Court-martialled for retreating, his defence was that he had maintained a 'fleet in being'. Undefeated, and still somewhere nearby, its very existence made any attempt at invasion extremely foolhardy. Two years later the French force was defeated at the battle of La Hogue.

# Eastbourne

What is now mainly a seaside town was one of the first experiments in town planning. Old Town, formerly known as East Bourne, where you will find the bourne (river) to which the name refers, is a mile from the sea. Two small fishing settlements developed. Sea Houses faced the beach and South Bourne lay inland from it, but the main part of the town, with open spaces and wide streets lined with trees, dates from the early 19th century. It was planned deliberately to be a pleasant place to live and to visit.

The Martello tower and the Great Redoubt, part of a chain of defences on the south coast, date from the Napoleonic Wars and can be visited on the way to the start of your journey.

*Looking over Eastbourne, from near the eastern end of the South Downs Way, towards Pevensey Bay.*

*Lawn tennis tournaments have been held at Devonshire Park, Eastbourne, for more than a century.*

# 2 Eastbourne to Alfriston

*Bridleway section:* through Jevington and over Windover Hill
7½ miles (11.9 km)

**Ascent** 1,080 feet (330 metres)
**Descent** 1,230 feet (375 metres)
**Highest point** Willingdon Hill: 660 feet (200 metres)
**Lowest point** River Cuckmere: 3 feet (1 metre)

**Note: Horseriders usually start from Warren Hill car park 9 as there is nowhere suitable to un-box at the official start.**

From the same start point as the footpath section **A**, head north-north-west, hugging the treeline for 100 yards to a fingerpost, and then in a south-westerly direction up a grassy sunken track away from the town.

To the north there are wind-stunted evergreen holm oaks and the Way opens out on to a broad grassy track. As the holm oaks thin out to form a combination of ash and thorn scrub, you pass a tumulus on the edge of the trail at a junction of fire rides. Here a fingerpost points the way ahead.

Above the treeline, just before the brow of the hill, you come to a multiple path junction. The Way now heads north-west and is marked by another fingerpost. From here there are splendid views over Eastbourne and the sea. The Way is now an almost level broad green track just below the skyline with dense scrub to the east.

After a bridlepath junction the trail starts to drop down towards the road and you can see Warren Hill car park **9** in the distance ahead. As you reach the road, the bridleway has been diverted to loop around to a safe crossing point. Here a series of fingerposts directs you to where you have the best visibility of approaching traffic – nevertheless, take care! Once across, the Way goes briefly parallel to the road and then continues in a north-north-westerly direction on a grassy track that heads into and alongside the scrub. Take care here as the trail is not level and on such steeply cambered grass it can be somewhat slippery.

At a multiple junction of bridleways there is a South Downs Way fingerpost pointing northwards past a trig. point which stands on top of a tumulus. This is close to a concrete dew pond **10**, which has some welcome seating. Ahead you can just see the tree clump at Butts Brow.

Just before dropping down to the road, the Way narrows. There are bus stops to the west of your crossing point. Take care, as there is a blind bend to the east. Pass the clubhouse and head through the golf course on a broad, chalky track.

There are views down Ringwood Bottom to East Dean, with Friston water tower just visible on the skyline. The path can be 'greasy' when wet but is now improved with new surfacing. Go west of the gorse clumps at the end of the golf course. Here the Wealdway (Gravesend– Beachy Head) briefly joins the South Downs Way.

To get to Eastbourne Youth Hostel **11** follow the Wealdway down the scarp slope. From this junction the trail continues for a further half mile (1 km), going past another maze of fire rides.

Two or three parallel routes run along the scarp top and, depending on the weather, you can choose the shelter of the scrub or the more exposed westerly path with its broader views. Where the Way touches the head of Eldon Bottom there is a restored dew pond **12** and a trough.

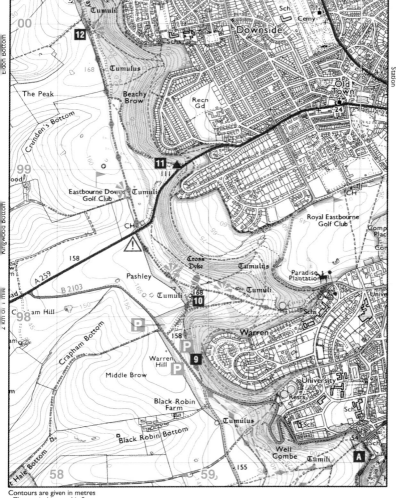

Contours are given in metres
The vertical interval is 5m

Head towards the trig. point on Bourne Hill above Jevington. This is a particularly good mountain-bike run with no gates.

Just south of the trig. point the Way heads west along a flinty, deeply rutted track. The views are into a wide, deep, dry valley, with the village of Jevington hidden in the trees below. There is an ancient crossroads here. Old Town Eastbourne, Willingdon and Jevington are signposted on stone plinths. These look like remains from a priory or a Roman villa but are actually part of an old Barclays Bank that was bombed during the war. The Way heads westwards to Jevington down a broad track between two sheep fences. It feels like an old coach road.

To the north, you can clearly see the lynchets of a Celtic field system **13** on the side of Willingdon Bottom and Coombe Hill. There are two tracks here separated by scrub, with the Way taking the more northerly route. You can pick out the square Norman tower of Jevington Church due west as you walk down Bourne Hill, and a series of tree clumps in the fields beyond.

It is sheltered here and the wind may be less biting. Coming down the Way into Jevington, you enter an area of ash trees with dark, overhanging branches. There are rabbit holes on the south side of this path and flint and tile cottages are visible down below.

Jevington Tea Gardens – open in summer – lie at the bottom of the track where you meet the road. At this junction, go north about 50 yards up the roadside, taking great care, and at the now closed Hungry Monk Restaurant (birthplace of Banoffee Pie) turn west again towards the church, where there is a water point. If you wish, go through the churchyard to the pub, past a tapsel gate hinged at the centre. These were designed to allow pallbearers carrying coffins to walk on either side.

At The Eight Bells, you can sit down by a fire in winter and thaw out. The row of walking boots in the entrance shows how popular the pub is with ramblers. On the way back, pause to visit the church before going north-westwards up a chalky bridleway. There are still a few elm trees here alongside the path as you rise to Jevington Holt and Holt Brow. The landowner once carefully fenced off the little islands of trees, which are a particular characteristic of this landscape, and hopefully they will flourish. At the western end of the fields you ascend more steeply underneath a canopy of trees. There is a mixture of elm, ash and horse-chestnut by the trail, but also a lot of exposed roots, so care is required at dusk.

*Ancient field patterns are still visible near Jevington.*

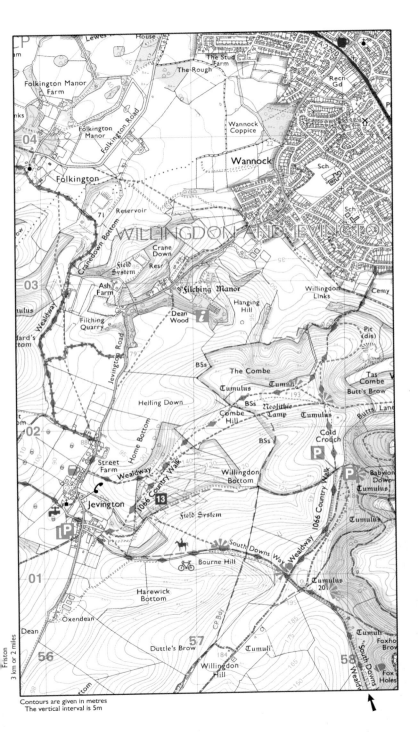

CP

Lewes

House

The Stud Farm

A2270

Folkington Manor Farm

The Rough

Recn Gd

04

Folkington Road

Folkington Manor

Wannock Coppice

Wannock

Sch

Folkington

WILLINGDON AND JEVINGTON

Sch

Reservoir

71

Cranedown Bottom

Crane Down

Resr

Field System

Filching Manor

Willingdon Links

Cemy

03

Ash Farm

Hanging Hill

Wealdway

Filching Quarry

Dean Wood

*i*

Pit (dis)

Jevington Road

BSs

The Combe

Tas Combe

Butt's Brow

Helling Down

Tumulus

Tumulus

Home Bottom

Combe Hill

Neolithic Camp

Tumulus

Butts Lane

02

BSs

Cold Crouch

Street Farm

Wealdway

1066 Country Walk

**13**

Willingdon Bottom

P

P

Babylon Down

Tumulus

Jevington

Field System

1066 Country Walk

Wealdway

Tumulus

P

South Downs Way

Bourne Hill

Tumulus 201

01

Harewick Bottom

CP Bdy

Oxendean

Dean

Tumuli

Foxho Brow

56

Duttle's Brow

57

Tumuli

South Downs

58

Fox Holes

184

Willingdon Hill

Wealdway

Friston
3 km or 2 miles

Contours are given in metres
The vertical interval is 5m

*The view across the Cuckmere Valley to High and Over and its White Horse from the South Downs Way at Windover Hill.*

About 550 yards (500 metres) out of Jevington the path levels off at a multiple bridleway junction. Your route crosses on one side of a triangle of nettles and small trees to a waymark post and up a broad track beneath more trees. The Downs to the north, once intensively cultivated, are now sheep pasture. Carry on westwards up to Holt Brow. As you reach higher ground, the path dries out and becomes chalkier.

On blustery days you can hear the wind beginning to roar in the trees as you gain height. At the top of the track, coming out of the woodland, there is a waymark post signalling your route north-west (right), while ahead another bridleway goes across Lullington Heath National Nature Reserve.

Pass through a narrow, scrubby section. After about 50 yards on the level you reach your first bridlegate, with stunted ash woodland to the north-east. After 380 yards (350 metres) you come to a second gate and you are now effectively on a sheep-grazed, rolling downland plateau, with views over Lullington Heath and north-west to Firle Beacon in the distance. To the north, on the edge of a very large arable field, is Hill Barn **14**, the remains of an isolated 'manure' barn. To the east you can see Beehive Plantation, the Neolithic camp at Coombe Hill, and on clear days Pevensey Bay. Head towards a post in the distance but do not be deceived by the sheep tracks.

To the south lie the 2,000 acres (800 hectares) of Friston Forest. Follow the waymarks north and then north-westwards towards the tumuli of Windover Hill. You can just see the cliffs of Newhaven and to the west the White Horse at High and Over. Before reaching Windover Hill, look south-westwards down the unspoilt dry valley of Tenantry

Ground **15** and Deep Dean – now Access Land under the Countryside & Rights of Way Act.

The Way passes through a wooden bridlegate and then curves round the top of Windover Hill **16** in a great arc along the route of an old coach road. The grassland is particularly good for downland flowers. From here, you can detour to the footpath above the Long Man **17**. This hill figure is best viewed from Wilmington, where there are the remains of a Benedictine priory, and a small car park with picnic site and public toilets. The depressions on the hill top, east of the Long Man, are all that remains of some Neolithic flint mines.

Descending to the Cuckmere Valley, you go through a bridlegate before passing the square outline of a water reservoir.

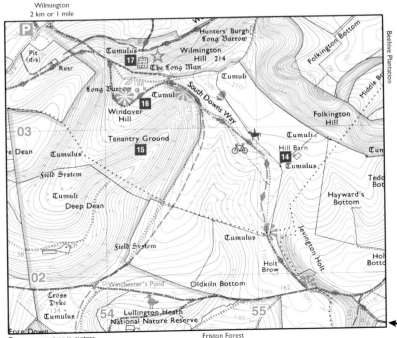

Contours are given in metres
The vertical interval is 5m

Berwick
1 km or ½ mile

Contours are given in metres
The vertical interval is 5m

*The old market cross in the centre of Alfriston.*

When the Way reaches the Litlington–Wilmington road, cross and continue down a wooded byway with a great arch of ash trees that offers shelter from the wind or shade from the sun. Join the Lullington to Alfriston road just east of Long Bridge.

At the bottom of this flinty track, cross another road and pass through a bridlegate in a post-and-rail fence. The Way turns southwards here, running inside the field parallel to the road towards Plonk Barn (now renamed Great Meadow Barn). After about 550 yards (500 metres), just off the floodplain of the River Cuckmere, proceed through another bridlegate. The bridleway and footpath sections merge here. Turn west and cross the white bridge into Alfriston. From here the Way goes briefly north on a gravel track and then up River Lane.

# The Long Man – an historical enigma

This splendid hill figure looking 'naked to the shires' is the largest representation of a human in Western Europe.

Until its restoration, the Long Man was visible only when there was light snow on the ground, or when the sun cast shadows into its shallow depression in the chalk grassland. In 1874 a public subscription was raised through *The Times* and the figure recut. The outline was probably 'sanitised' by the Victorians, as there are no known neuter figures in art history!

Many theories exist as to the date and purpose of the Long Man, varying from an Iron Age agricultural fertility figure to Alfred Watkins's view that he is a 'dodman' holding two posts for surveying and establishing ley lines. He also resembles the Anglo-Saxon god Baldur, or Christian figures seen on Roman coins.

As the earliest drawings of the hill figure are from the 18th century and no proof exists one way or the other, you are left to choose whichever theory suits you. From dowsing experiments over the Man, it is more likely to be a woman!

*The Long Man of Wilmington, tumuli and the South Downs Way on Windover Hill*

# 3 Alfriston to the A27 Crossing

*through Southease and Rodmell*

*13¾ miles (22.1 km)*

**Ascent**  1,830 feet (550 metres)

**Descent**  1,690 feet (510 metres)

**Highest point**  Firle Beacon: 715 feet (215 metres)

**Lowest point**  River Ouse: 3 feet (1 metre)

Before leaving Alfriston, you should visit the 14th-century Clergy House – the first property to be bought by the National Trust.

From The Star pub, go up Kings Ride. At the end, the Way becomes a flinty, chalk track, a drove road along which sheep were driven to market. As you climb you occasionally get glimpses down the Cuckmere Valley to Litlington and Friston Forest beyond. Behind you in the early-morning sun there is a wonderful silhouette of the Downs with Windover Hill dominating the landscape.

After a few hundred yards the Way levels off. There are smaller tracks leading to the north but your route goes straight ahead. The beautiful dry valley of France Bottom lies to the west. The track runs towards Long Burgh where it meets a multiple junction. There is a signpost directing you ahead and then another one a little further on.

As you travel along the ridgetop, views of the Weald stretch out to the north. To the south-west is the long arc of the Comp and due south the scrub of High and Over, with the river mouth at Cuckmere Haven beyond.

The Cross Dyke shown on the map must have been long ploughed out. The Way winds gently north-westwards, rising slowly towards Bostal Hill, passing a gate and another track heading north-east. A mile and a quarter (2 km) out of Alfriston you come to a bridleway gate where you cross over to the north side of the fence **A**.

Head north-west, closer to the scarp top and past the remains of a tumulus. Below, to the north-east, lie the woods of Firle Estate and the huge tithe barn of Alciston, a shrunken medieval village. To the west you catch the first glimpses of masts on Beddingham Hill. In the far distance, to the south-west, the little white lighthouse at the entrance to Newhaven Harbour is just visible on a clear day, and sometimes you will see the smoking funnel of the Dieppe ferry.

New Pond **18**, just to the north, and Jerry's Pond, to the south-west, are both dried-out dew ponds. Further west are more tumuli. Most of these ancient graves have been 'robbed'; you can still see where the Victorian 'digs' took place.

*The Great Tithe Barn at Alciston boasts the largest roof area of any tithe barn in England.*

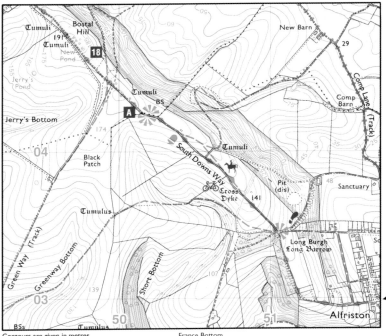

Contours are given in metres
The vertical interval is 5m

Pyramidal orchids are amongst the many varieties of orchid that grow along the South Downs Way.

and parascending clubs, who make use of the updrafts created by the steep slopes. In the summer the undisturbed grassland on this north-facing scarp slope is a good spot for the common spotted orchid. The Way heads northwest through a post-and-rail compound, past a little weather station, and then climbs gently towards Firle Beacon **19**. As you rise you start to see the white mast of the controversial Glyndebourne wind turbine to the north-north-west.

The Way now drops to Bopeep Bostal car park. This area is one of the favourite ridge-soaring sites for local hang-gliding

Stand on the tumulus for the best overall views. You can see Lewes to the northwest and Offham chalk pit beyond. Below to the north is the round Firle Tower – a folly that is a private house and part of

West Firle
1 km or ½ mile

BEDDINGHAM CP

The Lay

Coombe Barn

Elliman's Combe    Tumulus
Mill Mound          Beddingham Hill
Tumulus                              Cumuli
White Lion Pond      Radio Station      Males Burgh
                     **21**                Cumulus

**22**
**164**    Red Lion Pond

Settlement

Dook's Dyke

**05**

BSs

Cow Wish Bottom    Well Bottom

**45**

BSs
Tumulus
189
BSs

America Farm

170

160

143

135

128

115

P

**20**
Blackcap Farm    139

Blackcap Hill    134

**46**

Firle Bostal

Contours are given i
The vertical interva

Firle Estate, which has belonged to the Gage family since the 15th century.

From here the Way is almost level for about 2 miles (3 km). Up here the wind can blow so hard, and there is so little shelter, that your hands can go quite numb. To the south-west lies the bleak, isolated Blackcap Farm **20** and the first trees you have seen on the Downs since leaving Alfriston.

At the top of Firle Bostal go through a parking area and past the square outline of a water reservoir. In January you can find ewes here with blue backsides. These coloured marks, left by the ram, tell the shepherd how efficient it has been! North is the village of Glynde,

where John Ellman pioneered sheep improvement by breeding the famous Southdown in the 18th century.

Continue past the masts **21** and then north-west through a bridlegate and past a fingerpost. Piddinghoe Pond, sometimes dotted with the bright sails of windsurfers, lies to the south-west. You can see the trig. point next to Red Lion Pond **22** – now dried out. As you approach the brow of Itford Hill you overlook the Ouse Valley, with the villages of Southease, Itford, Northease and Rodmell beyond the river. The flat brooklands, drained in the 18th century, are criss-crossed by the straight lines of ditches. Asham pit, once a cement works

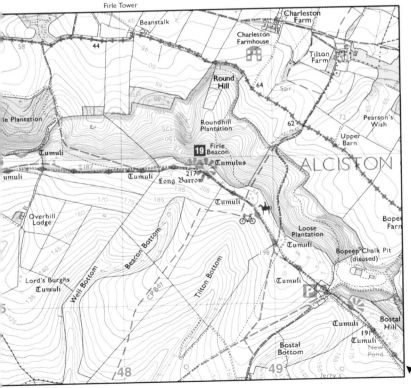

*Monk's House, Rodmell, home of Virginia and Leonard Woolf.*

and local tip, has now been restored to downland. Notice the sheep tracks around the contours of the nearby steep combe. To the north you can see the square tower of Beddingham Church and, beyond, Mount Caburn with its Iron Age hill fort.

Itford Hill is an excellent place for chalk downland flowers. You might find fairy flax, salad burnet and milkwort and, if you are lucky, pyramidal, common spotted, and bee orchids.

Due west is the round tower of Southease Church (see page 25) and Southease bridge crossing the River Ouse. As you descend, the Way curves southwards, parallel to the river, in a large loop that turns back along a farm track which heads downhill towards the A26 and Iford Farm. At the foot of the hill, where the track divides, fork left to cross the new bridge which carries walkers, cyclists and horseriders safely across the busy A26. On the far side of the bridge follow the track down to a T-junction at the entrance to the farmyard. Turn west here. (It is hoped a new Youth Hostel will open here in 2012.)

The tarmac lane leads you to Southease station. Cross the railway line via two gates alongside the level crossing. There are regular services – quite incredible for such a tiny halt. Continue west up the tarmac road to Southease, passing over the River Ouse, which is tidal at this point. In the past the bridge (recently restored by the Environment Agency) used to swing open to allow barges to carry their cargoes upstream to Lewes. You might spot dunlin, redshank and oystercatcher feeding on the mud at low tide. Occasionally cormorants rest on posts near the water's edge and herons stalk eels or frogs in the drainage ditches.

(Walkers wishing to access the facilities of Rodmell can either turn north along the footpath on the west bank of the river for approximately a mile (1.6 km), before turning west again along a bridleway track into the village or use the licensed footpath just east of the C7 road. These routes also offer the opportunity to visit Monk's House **23** (see page 66), where Virginia Woolf lived.

Alongside Southease Church is a conveniently situated bench and waterpoint, an excellent place to sit and rest. The unusual round Saxon tower and medieval wall paintings make this a special place to visit. From Southease, go up the hill to the Lewes–Newhaven road then north to a fingerpost in the verge along a narrow footway. Turn in a westerly direction at the fingerpost and (with care) cross the road to a hunt gate. Telscombe Youth Hostel can be reached from here either by travelling up the narrow road to the south-west, or along the new, safer National Trail route up Cricketing Bottom, for about 2 miles (3.2 km).

From the hunt gate on the Telscombe road, a waymark post directs you north-westwards down into Cricketing Bottom through another hunt gate and past a fenced gas-valve site. At the bottom of the hill turn south-west up the dry valley for about half a mile (800 metres) until, just before reaching a group of modern farm buildings, the route turns north-west.

After about 100 metres turn north through a hunt gate and up a steep hill, keeping beside the fenceline for some of the way. Take care to avoid the deep rabbit holes. The slopes at the top of this hill are a popular training site for paragliders and you may be lucky enough to see them practising.

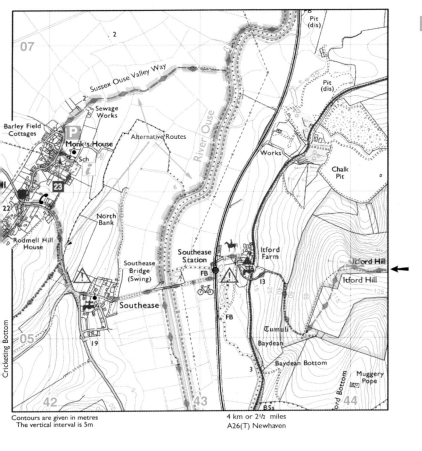

Cricketing Bottom

Contours are given in metres
The vertical interval is 5m

4 km or 2½ miles
A26(T) Newhaven

As you gain height, again there are views back over the Downs and on a clear day you can see the outline of Seaford Head and Haven Brow at the mouth of the Cuckmere. At the top of the hill you pass through a hunt gate. A signpost signals a bridleway down to Rodmell, and directs you north-westwards along the Way between trees and hedges. This narrow section of path, surfaced with clinker and ash from the village forge, opens out to magnificent views along the scarp and over the Ouse Valley to Lewes. Sadly, this townscape is now dominated by the tower block of County Hall rather than by the fine Norman castle. The strategic importance of Lewes can be clearly appreciated.

Continue north-westwards through a succession of bridlegates. At White Way you cross the Greenwich Meridian **24**, 0° longitude, and pass from the eastern global hemisphere into the west. Beyond, the concrete track between arable fields climbs the hill towards a barn on the skyline. Follow the waymarks round a short dog-leg, through a bridlegate along the edge of Swanborough Hill (see map page 63). Thirty yards north-west of a cattle trough lies a stone marked E.G. 26.12.59, a charming memorial which commemorates Mrs Greenwood, the mother of a local farmer.

### Southease Swing-bridge

The Grade II listed Southease Swing-bridge over the River Ouse is a rare example of this type of swing-bridge. It was designed by Henry E. Wallis, the engineer who also designed Brighton Station, and was constructed in 1880.

*Southease Swing-bridge spans the River Ouse.*

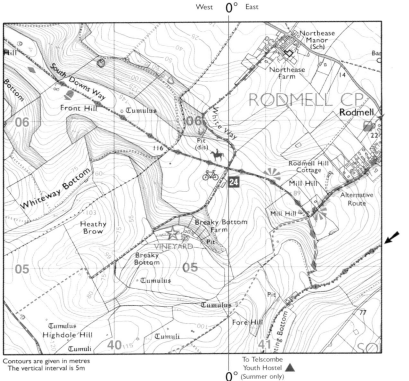

West  **0°**  East

Northease
Manor
(Sch)

Northease
Farm

Ba

**RODMELL CP**

Rodmell

22

South Downs Way

Front Hill

Tumulus

06

06

White Way

Pit
(dis)

116

14

Whiteway Bottom

24

Rodmell Hill
Cottage

Mill Hill

89

Mill Hill

Alternative
Route

Heathy
Brow

103

Breaky Bottom
Farm

VINEYARD

Pit

Mill Hill

Breaky
Bottom

05

05

Tumulus

Tumulus

Pit

Fore Hill

77

Tumulus
Highdole Hill

40

Tumuli

Tumuli

41

SO

Contours are given in metres
The vertical interval is 5m

**0°**

To Telscombe
Youth Hostel ▲
(Summer only)

Descend gently towards Kingston Hill dew pond **25**. Pass just to the south-west, but if you need shelter from biting wind, nip behind the nearby scrub. A little further north-west along the Way there are two more ponds and, next to these, you pass through a metal gate. To the west lies the spaceship-like structure of the new Brighton & Hove Albion football stadium. If you want to detour to Lewes, go north-east down the scarp slope towards the mock 18th-century, white postmill above Kingston.

Overlooking the spectacular, sheep-grazed Cold Coombes to the north, the Way runs south-west for about half a mile (0.8 km). This section of the trail is part of 'Juggs Road', an ancient route used to carry fish to Lewes market. The fish were kept fresh or salted in pottery jugs – hence the name. At the gas-pressure-reducing station, with its white wind turbine, head north-west towards the storm-damaged beeches of Newmarket plantation **26**. Here the Way turns north-east and runs down towards the A27, but, thanks to a realignment, it

*The home of Brighton and Albion Football Club, East Su*

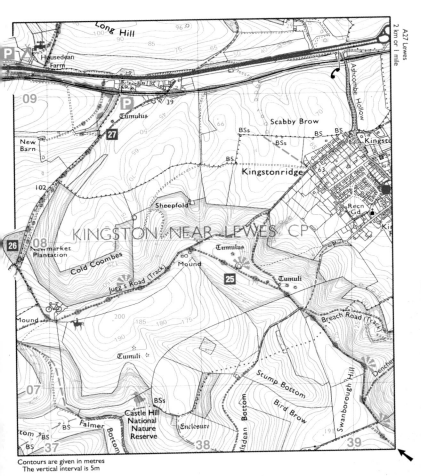

Contours are given in metres
The vertical interval is 5m

is no longer necessary to risk life and limb crossing the busy dual carriageway. About half a mile (0.8 km) downhill from the lower edge of the plantation, where the track jinks slightly to the east, go through a bridlegate on the left **27** and turn north on the track, which shortly leads to a metal gate at the top of a steep, wooded bank (take care descending). At the foot of the bank turn north-east and follow the edge of the field down to the railway.

When you reach the railway, turn west through another gate and, after about 75 yards, turn north under the bridge. On the far side of the bridge turn west and continue along a fenced path at the foot of the embankment. At the end another gate leads out onto a tarmac lane. Continue straight ahead up the hill and at the top turn north to cross the bridge over the A27. At the T-junction on the other side turn east and walk down towards Housedean Farm. From here you can walk or cycle into Lewes alongside the road, though the 2½-mile (4 km) journey is a noisy one.

Contours are given
The vertical inter

# A cultural circular walk or ride

*8¾ miles (14 km)*

There are three places of interest connected with the Bloomsbury Group in this area: Berwick Church, Charleston and Monk's House. All are just a little distance from the Way.

For a circular tour to Berwick Church and Charleston come north off the South Downs Way at Long Burgh above Alfriston and curve down eastwards to Sanctuary. Here turn north again along

the old Alfriston–Lewes coach road, past the recently converted Comp Barn. Just before reaching New Barn turn north-east to Berwick village and the church. After viewing the interior paintings, retrace your route to New Barn. At Alciston you might wish to divert briefly and look at the medieval tithe barn, then continue north-westwards along the coach road for 1 mile (1.6 km), before turning north-east to Tilton Farm. From here, turn west along a concrete farm track to Charleston Farm, once the summer retreat of the Bloomsbury Group and now open to the public.

From Charleston, continue westwards just south of Firle Tower folly to Heighton Street. From here turn south to rejoin the old coach road, briefly west again for about 200 yards and then up the scarp slope to rejoin the South Downs Way.

There are car parks at Bopeep picnic site, Alfriston, Charleston and a very small one at Berwick Church, where you could start this circular trip. The whole route is a bridleway, so riders, walkers and cyclists can enjoy it.

*Firle Tower folly, built in 1819 for Lord Gage's gamekeeper.*

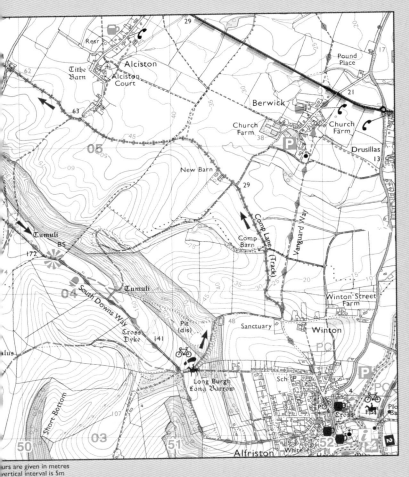

urs are given in metres
vertical interval is 5m

# The Bloomsbury Group in Sussex

The Bloomsbury Group was a group of English writers, artists and philosophers who met between 1907 and 1930 in the Bloomsbury district of London to discuss aesthetic and philosophical questions. Nearly all had been at Trinity or King's College, Cambridge. Members of the group included Leonard and Virginia Woolf, writers and founders of the Hogarth Press; Clive Bell and Roger Fry, the art critics; Duncan Grant and Vanessa Bell, the painters; Lytton Strachey, the biographer; and John Maynard Keynes, the economist.

*Virginia Woolf*

# Monk's House, Rodmell

Monk's House **23** was the home of Leonard and Virginia Woolf from 1919. Located on the winding village street, it is a modest brick and flint dwelling, now owned by the National Trust, with a rambling garden backing on to the walls of the churchyard. From this house Virginia, overcome by mental illness, walked towards the River Ouse and her suicide in 1941. The small, low rooms contain examples of the decorative work of Vanessa Bell and Duncan Grant in the form of painted tiled fireplaces, decorated furniture and ceramics.

(Open April to end October, Wednesday to Sunday, 1–5.30 pm (last admissions 5 pm), £4.20 (children £2.10, family £10.50). ☎ 01273 474760.

# Charleston farmhouse, Firle

Charleston farmhouse was 'discovered' by Virginia and Leonard Woolf in 1916 and subsequently rented by Virginia's sister, Vanessa Bell, as a country retreat. For decades it was to be occupied by painters and writers of the Bloomsbury Group. Life was bohemian and unconventional, an outpost of cultural and intellectual activity in the Sussex countryside.

Charleston is unique for its remarkable interior. It houses the most important remaining domestic work of painters Vanessa Bell and Duncan Grant. Textiles, pottery, carpets and wall paintings adorn each room with their characteristic flower and figure motifs.

*Duncan Grant*

When the last tenant, Duncan Grant, died in 1978, aged 93, the house was left in a sad state of repair. The Charleston Trust was formed to purchase, restore and preserve the house, its contents and garden for the future. It was opened to the public in the summer of 1986.

(Open: April to the end of October on Wednesdays, Thursdays, Fridays, Saturdays (guided tours only, 1–6 pm; last tour 5 pm), Sundays and Bank Holiday Mondays (Freeflow 1–5.30 pm; last admission 4.30 pm), price £9 (OAP concession Thursdays only, £8). ☎ 01323 811265 or visit www.charleston.org.uk.

*Vanessa Bell*

*Berwick Church, its interior painted by Duncan Grant, Vanessa Bell and Quentin Bell.*

# Berwick Church

The Church of St Michael and All Angels at Berwick contains extensive decorative work by Vanessa Bell, Quentin Bell and Duncan Grant. The small rectangular interior is dominated by the rich, flowing colours of four major murals, the flower-motif pulpit and numerous smaller paintings in the loose and characteristic 'Bloomsbury style'. Commissioned in 1941, they were installed with some opposition to their 'modern' nature. Much use was made of local figures and settings. A soldier and airman from Firle and a sailor from Berwick kneel respectively. The Nativity scene is set in Tilton barn with Firle Beacon in the background.

# Lewes

Lewes's name derives from the Anglo-Saxon word *hlaew*, meaning hill, and there has been a settlement here since Roman times. The town dominates the strategic downland gap cut by the River Ouse. All roads, railways and canalised sections of river pass this point.

The Saxons established a coin mint to encourage trade by land and water and this commercial function was reinforced by the Normans, who built the town's castle and priory.

In 1264 the King of England, Henry III, was defeated by Simon de Montfort at the Battle of Lewes and one of the first representative parliaments was established. The town later stood for religious freedom, as local Protestants had been burned at the stake (now celebrated on 5th November). In the 18th century Tom Paine, author of *The Rights of Man*, developed his republican views in the debating club at The White Hart.

To wander the streets looking at architecture ranging from Saxon to Georgian, and to explore the narrow 'twittens', is a relaxing change from tramping the bare downland. The town has a good variety of shops, places of interest, antique markets and public gardens. Harvey's, the local brewery, also makes an excellent range of beers.

# 4 A27 Crossing to Pyecombe

*past Ditchling Beacon and Clayton Windmills*

*8½ miles (13.5 km)*

**Ascent** 1,060 feet (320 metres)
**Descent** 860 feet (260 metres)
**Highest point** Ditchling Beacon: 815 feet (245 metres)
**Lowest point** Housedean Farm: 150 feet (45 metres)

At the foot of the tarmacked track leading down from the bridge over the dual carriageway you emerge onto a disused section of the old road in front of Housedean Farm. Where the road bends to the south opposite the farm gate continue straight ahead along the cycle track (NCN 90) with the handsome flint wall of the farmhouse garden on your left. At the end of the wall turn north up a stepped ramp which leads through a gate onto a track heading up Long Hill. As you reach the crest the trees of Bunkershill Plantation come into view – a prospect now sadly disfigured by a telecommunications mast. A bridlegate leads into the trees and the track bears round to the north-west to run parallel to the western edge of the wood. After a steep, zig-zag descent (take care if on a mountain bike or on horseback) you emerge into the open at the bottom of a shallow valley alongside an electricity pole transformer.

The fenced path leads north-east towards a clump of hawthorns on the hill opposite, where you turn to the east up the bank before continuing north-eastwards up the hill with a hedge on your right and a fence on the left. At the crest of the hill, where

you come to a T-junction, turn north-west. Ahead, to the north, you can see the tree clump of Blackcap, below which lies the woodland of Ashcombe Bottom. This rolling downland landscape was previously arable but is now grazed by sheep due to the success of agri-environment payments and the aquisition of Blackcap by the National Trust. To the west and north-west the sun casts shadows on the ridgelines of the huge Celtic field system of Balmer Down **28**. After passing through a pair of hunt gates, follow the stony track north-west towards the pylons.

About 100 yards after passing under the electricity lines the Way turns north at a waymark post, and after about 60 yards it is flanked by a thorn hedge. To the east you can see the converted grandstand of the old Lewes Racecourse. As you pass alongside the large rectangular plantation you will feel the benefit of its shelter. Take care to avoid deep ruts just north of the woodland – especially if cycling.

The Way turns sharply west along the ridgetop to Ditchling Beacon. There is a waymark here. Travellers going east could divert to Lewes. You now start to get magnificent panoramas.

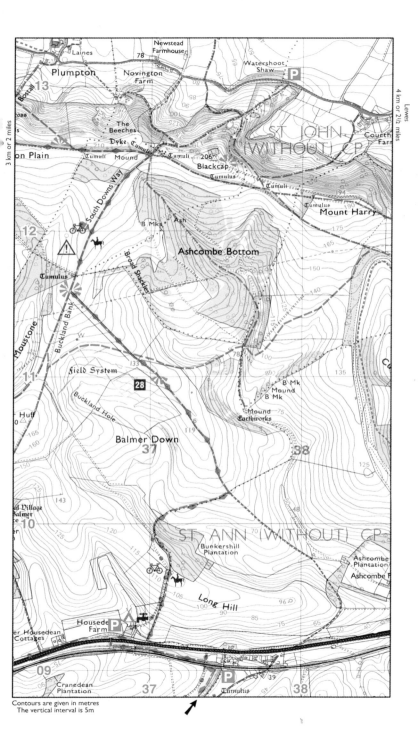

Contours are given in metres
The vertical interval is 5m

From Plumpton Plain the Way gently descends to Streathill Farm. In the scrub and trees to the south-west is a Bronze Age settlement **29**. You can look down to Ditchling and Westmeston. Note the wooded landscape of the clay Weald compared with the Downs. Just before reaching Streathill Farm a stony track leads down to The Half Moon pub.

North of the farm, the Way goes west across a tarmac road cut deeply into the Downs, and through a bridlegate. This is a sheltered spot to sit and have a drink. In summer, it is particularly good site for common spotted orchids. You might also see lots of snails. They need chalk to make their shells and are found in large numbers on old, unploughed downland.

The route runs through a long narrow grassland field. Just over the edge of the scarp slope you can see the tree tops forming part of a woodland 'V' **30** planted to commemorate Queen Victoria's Golden Jubilee in 1887.

Beyond Western Brow you pass an ancient deep track, and 550 yards (500 metres) further on there is a partially restored dew pond south of your route, just before you reach the Ditchling Beacon road. Cross with particular care. Go through the National Trust car park, where there is often a welcome ice-cream vendor and good views along the scarp of the Downs.

South of the main car park lie the ploughed-out remains of an Iron Age fort. In the north-western corner is a local interest information board.

Just to the west the Sussex Wildlife Trust has a nature reserve. You are free to wander down the slope to look at the flowers and butterflies. Of particular interest are likely to be orchids, including burnt, fragrant, frog, musk and bee. Fortunately, the botanical interest of this chalk grassland site is improving because of increased grazing, and the area is no longer being invaded by scrub.

Ditchling
1 km or ½ mile

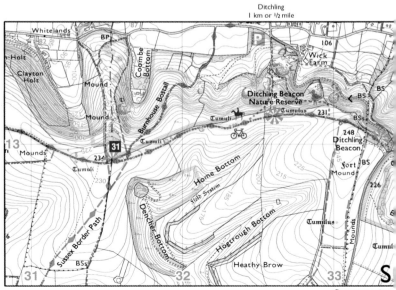

Contours are given
The vertical interv

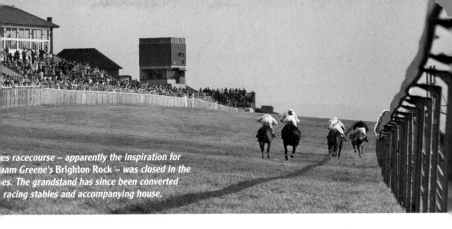

*...es racecourse – apparently the inspiration for ...am Greene's Brighton Rock – was closed in the ...es. The grandstand has since been converted ...racing stables and accompanying house.*

There is a trig. point in the centre of the hill fort and the remains of a viewing platform, from which thieves have stolen the brass direction finder and even the bricks. But no one can steal the view to the west towards Wolstonbury Hill, beyond to Devil's Dyke, and on a clear day as far as Chanctonbury Ring.

From this high point you gently descend towards Keymer Post **31**. The Way here has an open feel. There are constant views northwards to Burgess Hill and the densely populated area of mid-Sussex. On leaving the reserve, the Way continues on the level westwards, past two dew ponds – one dried out and one restored. By the westernmost pond, go through a bridlegate. Climb gently through a field of thistles on a broad track past some large dung piles.

At the brow of the hill is another bridlegate. Just to the west you reach Keymer Post **31**. Here, you pass into

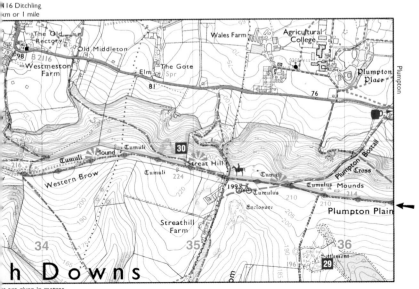

West Sussex. You can just see the sails of one of the 'Jack and Jill' windmills **32** peeping above the skyline, and Wolstonbury Hill, almost isolated from the rest of the downland, with dry valleys on either side.

After half a mile (0.8 km) turn sharply south through New Barn Farm. Here it is worth a detour to visit Clayton Windmills **32**. 'Jack' is privately owned; 'Jill', the small white post mill, is open, Sundays and bank holidays, May to September, 2–5 pm. About 100 yards beyond the farm turn west again. In the deep dry valley below you can see Pyecombe. In autumn there are hundreds of noisy rooks feeding on the stubble. The collective name for rooks is, appropriately, a 'clamour'.

As in East Sussex, the main route indicators are oak fingerposts with blue arrows. The Way continues westwards through a bridlegate alongside Pyecombe Golf Course. This track can be heavily cut up by horses and is obviously very well used. Near the clubhouse the Way passes the car park and drops to the road. Cross carefully. The trail then runs south behind a thorn hedge. This is a narrow, rough-surfaced section – difficult for riders. At a fingerpost you go south-west into Pyecombe village along School Lane. Riders and walkers should take care as there is no pavement.

*Jack (the black tower mill) and Jill (the white post mill), above Clayto*

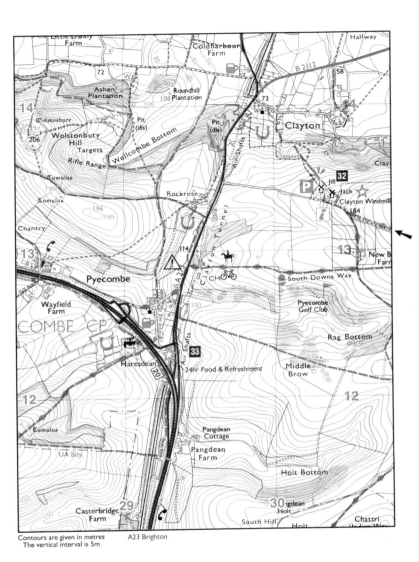

Contours are given in metres   A23 Brighton
The vertical interval is 5m

Pyecombe has a square, squat-towered Norman church. The inside is plain but with an unusual lead font. From Church Lane you can see the circular air-shaft towers **33** of the London–Brighton railway to the east if you pass down the lane towards The Plough Inn. The pub warmly welcomes walkers, especially if they remove muddy boots! Just south is a 24-hour M&S shop/café/toilets/ATM.

The bus stop for Brighton (15 minutes' journey time) is near the café. On the western side of the dual carriageway is a cycleway (NCN 20) linking Crawley and Brighton.

From Newtimber Hill the Downs-foot village of Poynings can be made out, with the aerials at Truleigh Hill and Chanctonbury Ring in the background.

# 5 Pyecombe to Upper Beeding

*passing Devil's Dyke and Tottington Barn Youth Hostel*

*7 miles (11.3 km)*

**Ascent** 1,030 feet (310 metres)
**Descent** 1,380 feet (415 metres)
**Highest point** West Hill (Newtimber): 680 feet (205 metres)
**Lowest point** River Adur: 3 feet (1 metre)

Start from Pyecombe Church and go north-west down Church Hill to a road bridge over the A23. After crossing the bridge, go southwards parallel to the main road and then westwards up a concrete track past Brendon's Horse & Rider Centre. Continue through a wooden bridlegate and past a nearby water trough. Start climbing the hill from this point up a broad chalk and flint track. The traffic noise can still be quite loud here, but there are fine views back towards the squat tower of Pyecombe Church and the windmills beyond.

There are two farm tracks (not shown on the map) leading off to the south and west; the Way curves up the hill in a south-westerly direction. There are a number of deep ruts alongside the route, which indicate that it has been used for hundreds of years, perhaps as a drovers' road. Higher up, there are signs of gulley erosion, with the bedrock of chalk exposed where the topsoil has been washed away.

## A Tapsel Gate

Pyecombe, famed for producing shepherds' crooks, has an interesting church 'tapsel gate', unique to this part of Sussex. The central pivot allows coffin-bearers to pass either side and rest the coffin on the gate. The handle is an example of a Pyecombe hook once made in the old forge opposite.

Pass through a wooden bridlegate next to a field gate halfway up the hill, and proceed to a waymark post on the horizon. Looking back, the views are tremendous. You can see the flat-topped outline of the quarry spoil heaps on Wolstonbury Hill. Numerous mountain-bike tracks indicate the growing popularity of this sport.

A dew pond shown on the map is buried in scrub to the east. The Way once drifted from the definitive route here, but you still head in a westerly direction along the main track. A smaller track straight ahead is now marked as a right-of-way on the map. To the south you can just see the tower blocks of Brighton and the coastal conurbations.

At the summit of West Hill there is an oak waymark post next to a wooden bridlegate and National Trust sign. Westwards lies the deep dry valley of Devil's Dyke (see map on page 79) and in the distance the four masts on Truleigh Hill. Pass through the gate and drop down towards

Saddlescombe Farm. The pasture underfoot is pleasant to walk on, less sticky than bare ground in the winter and softer going for horses. At the western corner of this field, where you meet another bridleway coming from the south, curve down to the farm through a wooden bridlegate and along a narrow, wooded track. The path deepens, and at the bottom of the track you pass a squeeze stile and signpost to Saddlescombe Donkey Wheel. Go through another bridlegate on to a short section of the route, which lies on a raised dry track, avoiding the main farmyard and past the Hikers' Rest café.

This new facility is open six days a week, March to November, 11 am–4 pm weekdays, 11 am–5 pm weekends; closed Wednesdays. From November to mid-December it is open Friday, Saturday and Sunday, 11 am–4 pm. The farm building,

which looks like a granary, houses the donkey wheel once used to draw water from the 4–5-metre deep farm well. You can visit this interesting relic – like a giant hamster's exercise wheel, as Saddlescombe is now owned by the National Trust.

Back on the Way there are a number of fingerposts pointing through the hamlet. After passing through a wooden field gate the lumpy track descends to the road and another wooden bridlegate. Care should be taken crossing the road here, as the traffic is fast.

Go up the steep, flinty track past a large ash tree. About 100 yards from the road the main track curves sharply round to the south-west, past the reservoir with an iron-railing fence. The definitive route of the South Downs Way has been diverted to this track north of the reservoir and

A23(T) Albourne Street
4 km or 2½ miles

A273 Hassocks
3 km or 2 miles / 24hr Food & Refreshments

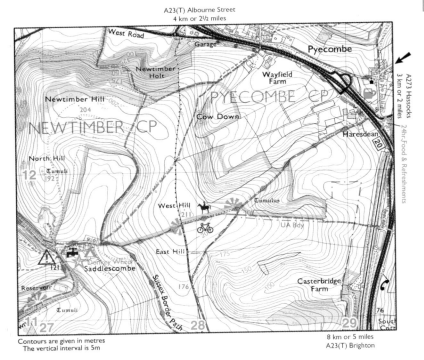

Contours are given in metres
The vertical interval is 5m

8 km or 5 miles
A23(T) Brighton

resurfaced with sandy Fittleworth stone. New waymark posts have also been added and the path passes through a mixture of scrub woodland and grassland. In summer look out for meadow brown, speckled wood, chalkhill blue, and adonis blue butterflies as you climb towards the Dyke Hotel through this mixed downland habitat.

Near the top of the hill you overlook the impressive deep dry valley of the Devil's Dyke **34**. (Why not make a brief diversion to further explore its flora and butterflies?) This is a long, gentle climb and you can just see the trig. point through the thorn trees.

The Way meets the road leading to the hotel but crosses to a wooden bridleway

*The deep dry valley of Devil's Dyke was probably cut when the ground was permanently frozen in the Ice Age.*

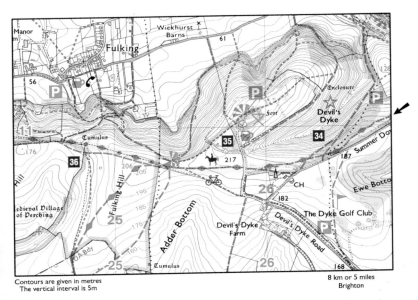

Contours are given in metres
The vertical interval is 5m

8 km or 5 miles
Brighton

gate. It is worth a walk up the roadside path to the Dyke Hotel, either for refreshments or for the stunning views. Inside there are now only a few interesting old photographs of the area: there used to be an aerial ropeway crossing the Dyke, a steam railway coming up from Brighton, and the place was more popular in Victorian times than it is today!

The quality of the views over the Weald varies from brilliant clarity to an eerie, low-lying mist clothing the landscape. The scarp slope stretches to the west and below lies the village of Fulking, with its sheep-washing spring dedicated to Ruskin. There are often colourful groups of hang-gliders and paragliders preparing to take off or flying along the ridge.

Rejoin the South Downs Way heading westwards towards the masts on Truleigh Hill. Follow the worn track across the middle of the level field and carry on westwards to the corner, where you pass through a metal bridlegate. The Devil's Dyke Iron Age fort **35**, which took advantage of the natural features, is best viewed by looking east from here.

From Fulking Hill you can see the Way undulating and winding westwards, and can just catch glimpses of Edburton Church at the foot of the Downs. This is an excellent stretch for mountain bikers.

Pylons march across the Downs here – hopefully one day the electricity lines will be put underground. Above Fulking you meet a number of deeply cut bridleways coming up the scarp slope. The little scrubby area in the field to the south marks the remaining foundations of Fulking Isolation Hospital **36**, used for people with contagious diseases. The definitive route of the trail briefly passes through this field, just between the remains of the hospital and the fenceline.

79

Pyecombe to Upper Beeding

From Perching Hill at 580 feet (177 metres) you descend steeply under the powerline that crosses this notch in the Downs and heads up towards Edburton Hill. It is just possible to see the remaining outline of a motte and bailey castle **37** on the skyline. Just as you pass under the line there is a metal bridlegate adjoining a field gate. A sign indicates that the National Trust owns Fulking Escarpment, which is an excellent site for downland flowers and insects.

The Way is now a broad, flinty track through huge grass fields rising gently around the south side of Edburton Hill.

The lack of background noise, and the open treeless landscape, allow sounds to carry great distances. Curve down to a second notch in the Downs above Edburton village, where the views to the north are rediscovered but lost again when you start to climb Truleigh Hill.

The arable fields have been converted back to rolling grassland – grazed by cattle. Without fencing, it could be open range! At the edge of the scarp there is a fingerpost indicating that a bridleway and footpath lead down the escarpment. It is worth diverting briefly to look at the ancient chalk grassland, which contrasts with nearby 'new grass' farming. This low spot offers some shelter.

Then you begin to climb Truleigh Hill. The Way passes just to the south of Truleigh Hill Barn and alongside an ugly cluster of masts, buildings, sheds and

fences. The views are south towards the coastal sprawl of Shoreham and Worthing. It is so bleak here that newly planted trees struggle to grow.

From Freshcombe Farm you have a gentle downhill run into the valley of the River Adur. Just below the brow of the hill is Truleigh Hill Youth Hostel, surrounded by pines. Although it looks like a landscaped office block, it is actually a converted 1930s summer house. There is a water point here. Bed and breakfast and evening meals are available, and the hostel is well equipped and even offers a vegetarian menu.

Just to the west, the track becomes metalled and is a fast downhill run for cyclists, although a bridleway running parallel to the Way provides a softer route for horses.

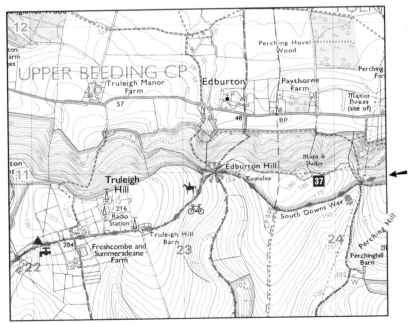

Contours are given in metres
The vertical interval is 5m

Pyecombe to Upper Beeding

NORTH LANCING

Garage

Golding Barn
Farm

Room Bottom

Windmill Hill

Quarry

**21**

**22**

Castle Town

New House
Farm

**10**

156

Cultivation
Terraces

27

Resr

**P**

South Downs Way

Beeding Hill

The War

16

**A**

**P**

168

160

Shoreham Road

Anchor Bottom

124

150

146

**09**

**09**

Passies
Pond

Quarry
(disused)

115

100

Chy

Works
(dis)

90

75

CP Bdy

Erringham
Farm

83

**08**

**08**

104

Chapel
(rems of)

Old Erringham
Farm

Downs Link

**P**

Mill Hill

67

Mill Hill
Nature Reserve

**07**

**07**

NTL

**222**

Steyning Rd

A283

BPs

Resr

**ADUR
DISTRICT**

Bucking
Barn

**P**

**P**

College
Farm

CHAPEL

Coombes Road

College Road

Contours are given
The vertical interv

Surrounded by sheep on the Downs here the views westwards can be obscured by mist, but, on a good day, are quite superb and you can clearly see the clump of trees at Chanctonbury Ring. The contrast between the valley and the Downs makes these hills feel quite mountainous. As you reach Beeding Hill the sound of traffic intrudes again. The chimneystack of the cement works peers over the line of the Downs, and to the south the chapel of Lancing College reaches skywards, its Gothic spires just visible.

Just below Beeding Hill and a mile (1.6 km) west of the youth hostel, there is a six-way path junction and a small car park. Do not follow the main track here, but pass through a bridlegate where a signpost indicates the way ahead into a large pasture field. The Way runs south-west above a deep dry valley called Anchor Bottom. You can see the shadows cast by the meadow ant hills on the far side of this valley, and ridges created by the cattle walking around the contours. Below lies the River Adur in its flood embankment, not far from the roundabout **A** and traffic of the A283. The Way continues through a bridlegate. Descend gradually into the valley on a chalky track with fenced arable fields on the south side. Cyclists should take care to avoid hitting the large flints on the surface of the path. At Castle Town, you can see a mock medieval château, which is actually a convent school.

Where the Way meets the main road, go southwards towards the little bridleway bridge over the River Adur.

From here there are buses going both north and south. These are 'request' stops, so remember to indicate to the driver by waving your hand that you wish him to stop.

*...ding Hill.*

# Dew ponds – a downland enigma

As you travel along the ridgetop of the high, dry Downs you occasionally pass shallow, saucer-like depressions of either puddled clay, chalk or concrete, which are the damp or dried-out remains of 'dew ponds'. In the heyday of downland sheep farming, before the invention of plastic water piping, there were literally thousands of these ponds between Beachy Head and Winchester. Their purpose was to supply drinking water for sheep, but an elaborate mythology has developed around them because few people were able to understand why they often held water in even the driest summers.

The name 'dew pond' is recent. Over 150 years ago they were called 'sheep ponds', 'mist ponds', 'fog ponds', or 'cloud ponds', and these hint at their true nature.

The first of the ponds may have been made by people who noticed that chalk or clay that had been trampled by cattle became watertight. The majority are lined with clay, to which a little quicklime was added to stop worm damage. Some ponds had straw mixed with the clay to reduce cracking in summer, and many had a layer of flints to protect the clay from penetration by animals' feet. All in all they are a fascinating and quite sophisticated piece of early engineering and, as the price of plastic piping rises and sheep are returned to the Downs, we may see more being reconstructed.

In the early 20th century, Edward A. Martin was given a grant by the Royal Geographical Society to undertake a series of experiments to discover the true source of supply to these ponds. Prior to these studies, which lasted more than three years, people believed that the ponds were replenished each night by

*This restored dew pond beside South Downs Way west of Ditch Beacon is still used to water livest*

dew. Interestingly, Martin found that there were very few occasions when the surface of the ponds was below dew-point and thus capable of condensing any airborne moisture. In fact, he estimated that the maximum annual dew-fall on the Downs does not exceed 1.5 inches (3.8 cm). Clearly, the main supply of water is from rain! The average annual rainfall on the high ridge of the Downs is 35 inches (89 cm), and the evaporation of water from the surface of the pond is approximately 18 inches (46 cm), giving a net gain of 17 inches (43 cm) over the whole area. Thus, when rain falls on the edge of the pond, some percolates into the ground and some adds to the water in the pond.

If you look at the shape of dew ponds, you can see that the actual rainfall collecting area is very large relative to the smaller evaporation surface. Martin inspected many ponds to see how they were constructed, and even built an experimental pond to see if it was possible to insulate the clay lining from the warming influence of the ground. He clearly proved that dew had almost nothing to do with filling these ponds. He also disproved the myth that they never dry up. He concluded that the rolling sea mists, low clouds and fogs of summer came to their rescue and helped to fill the ponds a little and, more significantly, to reduce the evaporation. Even in 1910 he bemoaned the fact that because farmers took them for granted, their failure to maintain them often led to cracking and plant-growth damage, so that the ponds dried up.

Nowadays, the few that still function, such as those on Lullington Heath and Chanctonbury Hill, have been restored by conservationists.

# 6 Upper Beeding to Washington

*via Steyning Bowl and past Chanctonbury Ring*

*6 ¾ miles (10.9 km)*

**Ascent** 860 feet (260 metres)
**Descent** 520 feet (155 metres)
**Highest point** Chanctonbury Ring: 770 feet (230 metres)
**Lowest point** River Adur: 3 feet (1 metre)

There is a small car park at the roundabout **A** on the Upper Beeding road suitable for horse boxing. From a barriered layby on the west side of the A283 the trail passes through a gap in the hedge. Beyond this go south, parallel to the main road, and then turn westwards between post-and-rail fencing to a bridle bridge over the river. At this point there is a picnic area, complete with trough, tap and hitching rail, provided by the Society of Sussex Downsmen (now the South Downs Society).

The river has tidal floodbanks either side with footpaths on top. Historically it was an important trade link and in the medieval period Bramber, a mile (1.6 km) upstream, was a significant port. The town even produced early Norman coinage.

At the other side of the bridge, go north-west alongside the river. Just to the west you can see the little church of Botolphs **38**. This is Saxon and lies in a hamlet near a timber-framed clergy house. The church has a Horsham stone roof and the hamlet is so small that it is indicative of a shrunken medieval village. The Way leaves the bank at a waymark post and crosses the floodplain of the River Adur on a raised bridleway. Watch out for cormorants, which you can sometimes see feeding in the river and in drainage ditches.

## Chanctonbury Ring

The ring of beech trees at Chanctonbury Ring was originally planted by Charles Goring in 1760. The trees were positioned within the ramparts of a small early Iron Age hill fort, which later became the site of a Roman temple.

Just before the road a fingerpost indicates the Way westwards, while the Downs Link path runs north along a disused railway line – and links the South Downs Way with another National Trail, the North Downs Way. Go through a gap in the fencing alongside the road and follow the field-edge bridleway in a north-westerly direction – it can be rather muddy in winter. Curve westwards on the road and pass by Annington Farm as you start to climb the western slopes of the Adur Valley. About 50 yards past Annington House (rear entrance) the Way turns south and leaves the tarmac behind, as indicated by a fingerpost.

Go up a broad farm drive with sycamore, ash and elm making a fine arch of trees in the summer. Just past the entrance to a house once curiously called 'Tinpots', turn south-west and start climbing up the Downs along a sunken, wooded lane towards a wooden bridlegate. There are distinctive blocks of trees planted in the dry valley of Winding Bottom, as well as a line of pylons. Head north-westwards, past the farm dung heap and a concrete floor slab – all that remains of a burnt-out modern barn. To the east you can see the huge disused cement works, and the River Adur meandering down to the sea.

The landscape is a mixture of arable and pasture, and the track is quite flinty ahead. As you climb there are views to the south and east over this beautiful valley. Follow the north side of the fence

as it curves round to head in a westerly direction. You start to get views over the upper Adur Valley and Weald. Below lies Bramber, with its Norman castle which was still of strategic importance during the Civil War in 1643.

The Downs are bare here, giving a sense of isolation. Approaching the western end of the field above Winding Bottom you can just see the road that leads from Bramber to Steyning around the head of Steyning Bowl. At a bridlegate the Way is waymarked westwards. Go past Bramber Beeches **39**, a triangular group of trees planted by the West Sussex Federation of Women's Institutes, and head for the skyline. There are splendid views into Steyning Bowl **40** (see map on page 89), a huge, dry valley or combe sometimes used for hang-gliding and paragliding.

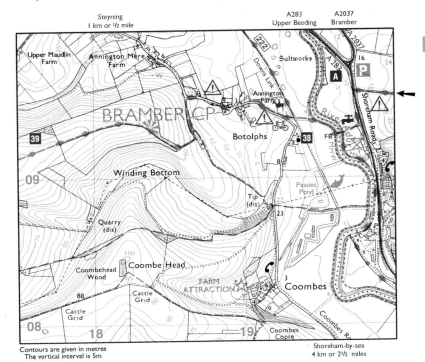

Contours are given in metres
The vertical interval is 5m

Shoreham-by-sea
4 km or 2½ miles

While quite pleasant underfoot for horses, this huge sheep pasture could be a little scary for riders if noisy model aircraft are being flown. Carry on westwards, with the fence on your north side. This open landscape is a good spot for a gallop past the gaunt outlines of wind-blown trees. When you reach the brow of the hill and the road, take some time to enjoy the broad views to the west.

The Way heads north, just east of the roadside fence, up a broad bridleway that is sometimes full of molehills. To the west, across a dry valley, you can see the ramparts of Cissbury Ring, which incorporates an Iron Age hill fort and Neolithic flint mines. The Downs feel plateau-like and can be very cool on a windy day. There is a paragliding and hang-gliding site at Steyning Bowl **40**, with splendid views east to Truleigh Hill.

At a point where the road turns north-eastwards, the Way is signposted between two metal posts. Great care is required in crossing the road. The Way then becomes a part-surfaced farm track heading towards a clump of scrub on the skyline. Go north across an arable field to another metal gate alongside which lies a memorial to Walter and Thelma Langmead – local farmers. At this multiple bridleway junction the route is signposted towards a trig. point. From here, if you wish, you could make a diversion down to Steyning to pick up supplies and visit this charming Saxon village, once a port, until the silting up of the River Adur in the 13th century. Steyning became popular last century with writers and artists – William Butler Yeats and James Whistler both stayed here. The Way here is a flinty track. As you approach the scarp edge you can occasionally see northwards to villages in the Weald. The woodland clumps have recovered from their raggedness, created by the great 1987 storm, and the slope is clothed in trees rather than downland grass.

From the trig. point you have a long ridgetop run ideal for mountain bikers and riders. Ahead to the west you can see the clump of beech trees which marks the Chanctonbury Ring Iron Age hill fort. On the bitterest winter days you can still meet parties of hardy local ramblers enjoying the fresh air, even singing Christmas carols as they walk along! Looking southwards down the dry Steyning Valley there are better views of Cissbury Ring in the distance.

At the westernmost head of the Steyning Valley there are the remains of a dried-out dew pond **41** with ash and thorn trees growing in its bed.

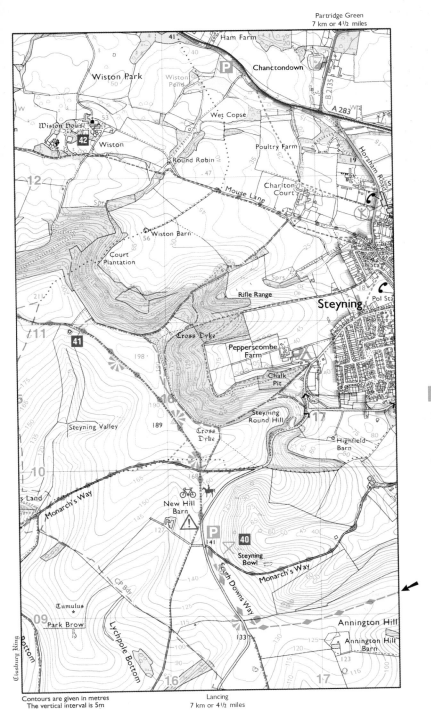

Ham Farm

Chanctondown

Wiston Park

Wiston Pond

Wet Copse

Poultry Farm

Wiston House

42

Wiston

Round Robin

Charlton
Court

Mouse Lane

Horsham Road

12

Wiston Barn

Court
Plantation

Rifle Range

Steyning

Pol Sta

Cross Dyke

41

Pepperscombe
Farm

Chalk
Pit

198

Steyning Valley

190

Steyning
Round Hill

17

Cross
Dyke

189

Highfield
Barn

10

Monarch's Way

New Hill
Barn

P

41

40

Steyning
Bowl

Monarch's Way

South Downs Way

Tumulus

09

Park Brow

Annington Hill

133

Annington Hill
Barn

Cissbury Ring

Lychpole Bottom

16

17

Contours are given in metres
The vertical interval is 5m

Lancing
7 km or 4½ miles

*Glancing over the scarp slope east of Chanctonbury the Elizabethan mansion of Wiston House can be espied.*

*Chanctonbury Ring, with its distinctive clump of storm-battered beech trees.*

It is difficult to make out the cross dyke and tumulus mentioned on the map as you pass through a wooden bridlegate beside a cattle grid. Many of the archaeological features mapped in the 1960s have been further damaged by continued ploughing. The Way passes a large water tank (for gravity-feeding cattle troughs).

The South Downs Way now curves gently to the south of Chanctonbury Ring **43**, famous for its clump of beech trees planted in 1760 by the young Charles Goring of Wiston. It is said that for months he carried water up the hill in bottles to aid their growth. When some of these trees blew over in the 1987 storm they revealed interesting Iron Age and Roman archaeological features and the site was properly excavated before replanting. There are magnificent views all around from this vantage point. Sometimes the mists below are thick enough to mislead children into thinking they are looking out over the sea.

Travelling west again you can see the trig. point of Chanctonbury Hill and the edge of a dew pond to the south. It is worth a brief diversion to the high spot to look north-west. Down below, at the scarp foot, you can see the contrasting geology of the sand pit at Rock Common.

Rejoin the trail and take the main track southwards towards Findon, passing through a bridlegate next to a cattle grid. Have a quick look at the dew pond, which was originally constructed around 1870, restored by the Society of Sussex Downsmen (now South Downs Society), then head along the main track, with

The still ragged outline of Chanctonbury Ring **43** is visible on the skyline to the north-west. On reaching the finger of woodland running up to the Way, you come to another signpost. Take the northernmost track rather than the bridleway to the south-west.

You pass a sheep-penning area by Lion's Bank, where the shepherd will mark and count his flock. You might just see Wiston House **42** (see map on page 89) and the surrounding parkland through the trees in winter. There is a multiple bridleway junction at the top of Chalkpit Wood and a fingerpost directs you towards Chanctonbury Ring **43**. The Way climbs gently as a broad trackway from here to 780 feet (238 metres) at the high point of Chanctonbury Hill, just a little west of the Ring.

the deep valley of Well Bottom to the south. Curve southwards to a fingerpost where you turn north-west.

The trail now descends with fences either side, and you see large sheep flocks grazing, rather than ploughed arable Downs. At the scarp foot lies Washington and you can begin to hear the traffic of the A24. Where the track winds its way into woodlands, you pass wayfaring trees, elder, hazel coppice and some oaks. Mountain bikers have to brake hard on the bends going down this steep, flinty track.

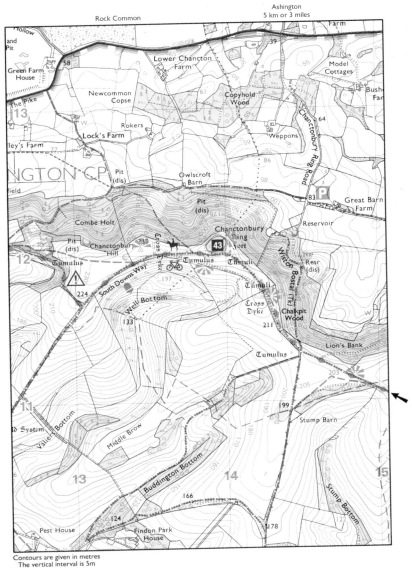

Contours are given in metres
The vertical interval is 5m

Upper Beeding to Washington

As you come out of the little wood there is some good chalk grassland to the north. Past the deserted farmhouse at Frieslands there is old man's beard on the bushes and garden escapes of cotoneaster among the natural downland species. The ground can be very sticky in winter, with your boots carrying large clods. Horses are best led.

On the descent you pass a gas-pressure-reducing station, the noise and smell of which bring you back to 'civilisation'. If you wish to visit the pub or shop in Washington, walk the safe footpath northwards just before reaching the car park.

Just beyond, the Way is signposted south to the A24, where it joins the little loop road to Washington. Do not take the track to the quarry. The trail goes directly across the dual carriageway here and *great* care should be taken.

However, it is a short walk up the side road to Washington and by going into the village all trail users can avoid the very dangerous A24 road crossing. At The Street turn west, go past the church and across a bridge over the A24. Continue to Rowdell House, where you turn briefly south past Home Farm **B** and then south-west up the scarp slope to rejoin the South Downs Way at Barnsfarm Hill.

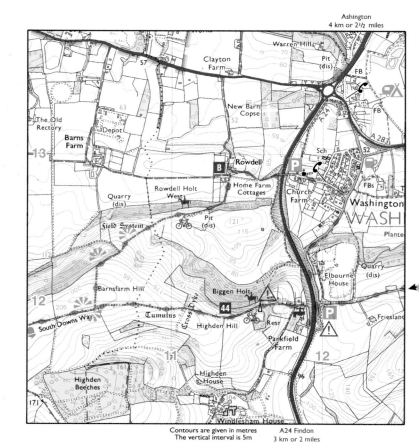

Contours are given in metres
The vertical interval is 5m

A24 Findon
3 km or 2 miles

# 7 Washington to Amberley

*past Chantry Post and Rackham Banks*
*6 miles (9.7 km)*

**Ascent** 540 feet (160 metres)
**Descent** 830 feet (250 metres)
**Highest point** Barnsfarm Hill: 670 feet (200 metres)
**Lowest point** Amberley (B2139): 30 feet (10 metres)

From the South Downs Way car park at Washington to the A24 there are a number of fingerposts directing you to a point opposite Glazeby Lane. Crossing the A24 is very tricky; the traffic is extremely fast and thunders by (see previous chapter for alternative safe crossing). Once across, there is a fingerpost: go north, parallel to the main road. Although once permitted, vehicles other than pedal cycles have now been prohibited from driving along the Way between Washington and Amberley, as the noise and disturbance spoilt the enjoyment of other users.

The lane starts with a verge wide enough for horses. After about 100 yards, it turns westwards and begins to climb a hill. There is a clearly marked water tap at this point. Opposite the entrance to Moo Moo Farm there is another fingerpost pointing westwards up the steep tarmac path. Horses might find this section a little bit slippery in frosty weather as there is no verge. Pass another fingerpost as you leave the tarmac over a motorcycle trap on to a flinty track. There is an ash hanger to

the north through which you can see the Weald when the trees are leafless.

There is a strange metal, asphalt and concrete bunker **44** almost at the top of the hill. It is an ugly building but an interesting piece of Britain's World War II defensive history, with gun ports pointing out over the Weald. Towards the top of Highden Hill, look back north-east to Washington Church, with its square tower, and note the contrasting geology between the quarries of the Lower Greensand and the chalk pits. You can see Worthing and the sea to the south. A thick, low-lying mist may limit the views, but not being able to see the towns enhances the overall feeling of isolation. You can occasionally see smoke rising from a woodland fire down in the Weald, but the village of Storrington to the north-west, so distinct on the map (page 99), is usually hidden by trees. To the south-east you get a clear but distant view of Cissbury Ring, even on hazy days.

The views from the top of Barnsfarm Hill (where the alternative route rejoins the Way) are primarily to the south, as you cannot see over the scarp slope.

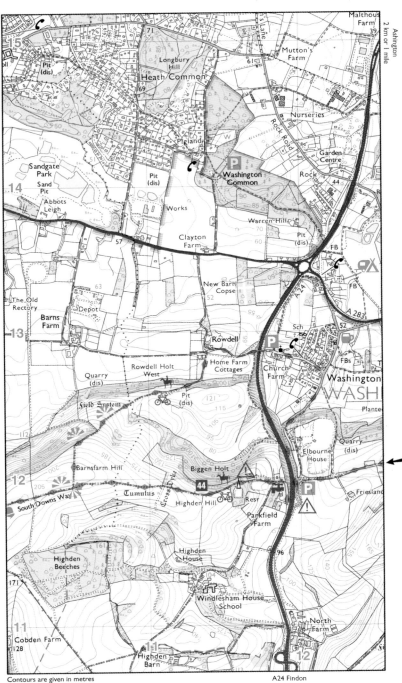

Contours are given in metres
The vertical interval is 5m

A24 Findon
2 km or 1 mile

*A quarry cross-section shows how thin the downland soils are.*

The track can be muddy here, but is level. A little further west, after passing through a bridlegate, the lines of the cross dyke, on the promontory of Sullington Hill, and of the trackway leading down to the scarp are obvious.

To the north you can see the shrunken village of Sullington, with a tiny Saxon church. In winter it can be cool up here, so you have to walk at a brisk pace to keep warm.

At the southern end of the bridleway, coming up the eastern slope of Sullington Hill, there is a multiple path junction with a modern Dutch barn and two cattle troughs. At the barn you pass through a bridleway gate. Beyond, the Way goes over a cattle grid, but there is a bridleway gate alongside for riders. Riders and cyclists should note that Chantry Post **45** car park is bounded by motorcycle traps on both sides. This is a favourite kite-flying spot and can be a great joy for children.

Just before the car park, the Way goes over another cattle grid and horseriders can pass through a wooden hunt gate alongside. Chantry Post **45** now has all its fingers, which is a great help for orientation. South is Harrow Hill with its enclosure marked on the top, and a superb line of trees to the west coming northwards from Lee Farm.

From the car park pass through a number of arable fields bounded by thorn trees. Just to the west, the path widens out. Take the track, which is hard and chalky, north of an almost dried-out dew pond.

On grey days, shafts of sunlight pick out patches of the Downs, more rolling and wooded as you go westwards, with pink light on the sea to the south. From the top of Kithurst Hill the Way runs down to

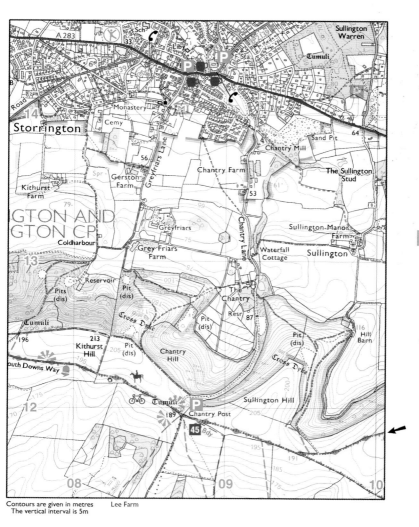

Contours are given in metres    Lee Farm
The vertical interval is 5m

another car park near Springhead Hill, with a fine clump of trees beyond. In this car park there is the white-painted Parham Post **46**, which helps visitors get their bearings.

The Way climbs gently westwards to Springhead Hill, on compacted chalk that can be a bit 'greasy' in wet weather. As you approach the top, the track becomes very flinty, but it is broad enough for horses to ride on the softer verge. Sadly, the copse here was badly damaged in the 1987 storm, but it is still a key landscape feature and there are some fine lichens and fungi beginning to grow on the rotting timber. Take the northernmost bridleway running along the scarp slope. There is a South Downs Way fingerpost here, indicating the route east and west and easily missed. The cross dyke marked on the map seems to have been ploughed out, but about 160 yards (150 metres) west of the beech copse there are still the remains of a plundered tumulus, surrounded by small thorn trees.

There are now fabulous views to the north over the Weald and Parham Deer Park **47**, with its house, woods, ponds and follies. The Way is now a rutted chalk track. The route is almost level, but gently climbs to Rackham Hill at 633 feet (193 metres). To the north you can see the River Arun winding through its water meadows.

Look out over Amberley Wild Brooks as you get towards Rackham Banks (see map on page 103). To the west lies Bury Hill and the Downs beyond, and on the valley floor to the north there is Rackham, with its little white and cream houses, and other villages in the distance.

The Way passes a trig. point at Rackham Hill. It used to be surrounded by scrub but is now a useful distance indicator. From here, descend gently westwards towards Amberley and Houghton Bridge. About 200 yards (180 metres) west of the top of Rackham Hill you

*Winter flooding in the water meadows of Amberley Wild Brooks.*

Pulborough
6 km or 3½ miles

West Sussex Literary Trail

Hill
Plat
Douglas's
Lodge

West Plain

Parham Park
(Deer Park)

**47**

Parham House

Windmill
Hill

Resr
(dis)

Cootham

Cootham
Farmhouse

Clay Lane

Amberley

**14**

Pope Lane (Track)

Woodmill
Pond

Ash Copse

Paddock
Wood

The Folly

Weirs

Paygate
Cottage

Rackham
Farm

Springhead
Farm

57

60

**STORRIN
SULLIN**

**13**

Pits
(dis)

Pit
(dis)

Rackham Banks

Earthwork

Tumulus

Cross
Dyke

Springhead
Hill

Tumuli

**P**

Tumuli

Tumulus

193

Rackham
Hill

191

172

**46**

180

**06**

157

165

**07**

**South Downs**

Contours are given in metres
The vertical interval is 5m

*The quarry railway at Amberley Working Museum.*

here is rather steep and stony, descending between fences to a wooden bridlegate. The Way is particularly tricky after the gate and it might be best to lead a horse. At the bottom of this short, difficult section join a road where a fingerpost points you westwards along the curved, metalled surface past a tile-hung house called 'High-down'. You quickly come to another fingerpost directing you south-west down a little road called 'High Titten'. There are good views into the chalk pit **49**, the bottom of which is quite wooded. As you walk down High Titten, with a broad verge suitable for horses, there is a bank of trees covered in old man's beard sweeping round the chalk-pit edge. Here there is a small informal campsite overlooking the quarry.

At the bottom of High Titten you meet the B2139 road. The Way goes north along the field edge and crosses the road just south of a flint barn. The nearby museum is well worth a visit. Access to it is gained via the footway on the opposite side of the main road – cross with great care. The museum entrance and ticket office are just inside Amberley railway station car park. There are regular services from this station and toilets on the platform (though they are sometimes padlocked).

Allow two hours to visit Amberley Museum (open from April to October). It has a narrow-gauge quarry railway, a printer's shop, a blacksmith's shop, stationary engines, many other displays and a museum shop plus restaurant. The pub next to the railway station, The Bridge Inn, welcomes walkers and offers bed and breakfast, and food, both lunchtimes and evenings. Nearby is a drinking trough and water tap.

cross the substantial, but little understood, earthwork known as Rackham Banks **48**.

About 50 yards west of some more tumuli at Amberley Mount there is a kissing-gate onto the adjoining access land and a wooden gate. Riders may have to dismount to open and shut this properly. The trail drops quite sharply to Downs Farm, where there is a wooden bridlegate with an iron field gate. Do not go into the farmyard but follow fingerposts due west. This once muddy section of the route has recently been resurfaced.

From Downs Farm you can just see the white face of Amberley chalk pits **49**, now an industrial museum. The route

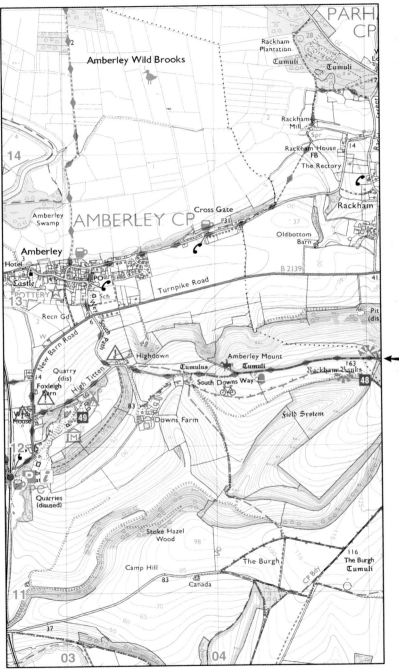

Contours are given in metres
The vertical interval is 5m

# 8 Amberley to Cocking

*past Toby's Stone and Crown Tegleaze*
*12 miles (19.3 km)*

**Ascent** 1,590 feet (480 metres)
**Descent** 1,300 feet (390 metres)
**Highest point** Crown Tegleaze: 770 feet (230 metres)
**Lowest point** River Arun: 3 feet (1 metre)

The South Downs Way has thankfully been diverted away from the dangerous roadside route through Houghton. The trail now runs due north parallel to the main road (B2139) towards Amberley village and away from the railway station and museum on a broad fieldside track. About 100 yards north of the junction with the road you come to a converted flint barn with a red clay-tile roof and fox windvane. Turn west and cross the road carefully, then turn north again on another section of new footway for another 100 yards. Then turn west down a concrete farm track and cross the railway. Go past the sewage works, with Coombe Wood ahead of you on the Downs across the valley. The farm track drops gently past a welcome waterpoint to the water meadows of the River Arun. At a metal field gate turn south and head towards the new bridle bridge over the river. To the south-east you can see the white scars of the Amberley chalk pits and to the west there is still the ragged outline of a storm-damaged woodland on the skyline.

You may be lucky enough to catch a glimpse of reed buntings nesting in the ditch alongside the farm track here, or to spot some 'horsetail' – a remnant prehistoric plant. Just before reaching the floodbank of the river, pass through a hunt gate and then turn west on this raised bank to the new bridle bridge. The river is tidal, so you may see it carrying occasional flotsam upstream, which can be rather disconcerting. At the far side of the bridge turn westwards along the floodbank for about 120 yards. Where the river turns north-east, leave the bank and drop down into the watermeadows, weaving your way alongside ditches and through several hunt gates to Houghton Lane. Here a fingerpost indicates the route westwards.

The Way is a broad, flinty track passing through arable fields towards a clump of trees. Your route turns north-west and then west again as you rise. From the viewpoint **50** you can clearly see the meandering River Arun in the water meadows; in winter, Bury Church is visible to the north.

It is a steep climb, past Coombe Wood – a mixture of ash and beech with some holly on the fringes. There are still huge fallen trees everywhere; their great upended root plates all facing south, a reminder of the 1987 hurricane.

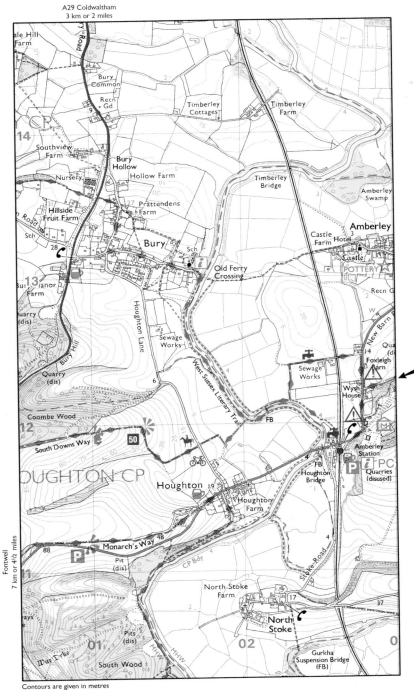

Contours are given in metres
The vertical interval is 5m

A29 Coldwaltham
3 km or 2 miles

Fontwell
7 km or 4½ miles

At the road junction a fingerpost points you north for about 100 yards. Cross carefully to a footway on the other side. The Way westwards is signalled by another fingerpost and you leave the road towards Houghton Forest and Bury Hill.

The path levels off as you reach the top of the Downs, where it meets a complex path junction **A**. Follow a fingerpost pointing you north-west. The Way rises gently towards Westburton Hill, and you can now see the radio masts between Sutton Down and Bignor Hill.

The huge expanse of Houghton Forest spreads out below to the south and west, giving a completely different character to the landscape. The Way becomes grassy – more comfortable underfoot for horses than the flinty track. You travel on the level, just off the scarp slope, along the contours. The only man-made feature

visible is the isolated structure of King's Buildings to the west.

There are lots of skylarks and, in winter, flocks of fieldfares. The peace is disturbed only by the occasional plane passing overhead and by the faint 'popping' of shotguns. Your route comes gently off the back of Westburton Hill, heading north-westwards, and drops into a 'notch' in the Downs. There is a group of barns that sometimes houses overwintering cattle. Stop in the shelter or shade to have a snack before climbing Bignor Hill. The track can be very muddy from farm-vehicle use. The wood to the west of the farm buildings has the wonderful name of Egg Bottom Coppice.

Just to the west there is a junction of paths. Follow the South Downs Way signposts south and then west again. The bridleway leading down to Bignor and Bignor Roman Villa is signposted here. The Way winds steeply through scrubby woodland and, at the edge of the ash scrub, you find another fingerpost directing you through a bridlegate and then north-westwards. King's Buildings are just visible to the south of this turn, with Houghton Forest beyond. After about 80 yards (75 metres) the track curves westwards again towards the top of Bignor Hill.

Due north you can see the woodland and house of Bignor Park and to the east even the clump of Chanctonbury Ring is visible. Toby's Stone **51**, now restored, bears an inscription to James Wentworth-Fitzwilliam, 'Toby', once secretary of the local hunt, and is a horse-mounting block. The Slindon Estate to the west is owned by the National Trust and open to the public. From Toby's Stone go west, climbing quickly past the top of Bignor Hill

*Skylarks can be heard and spotted along much of the South Downs Way.*

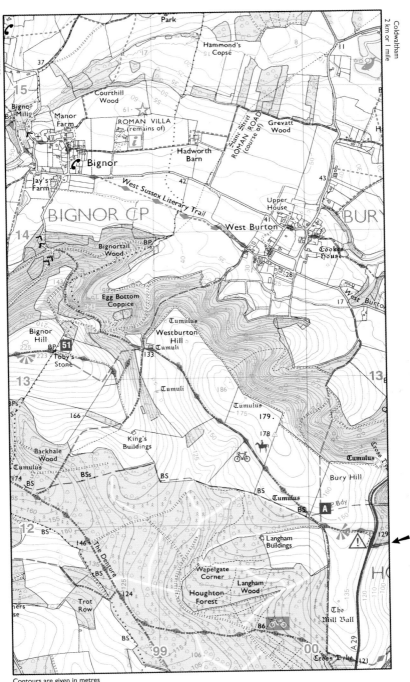

Sutton

Park

Hammond's Copse

37

15

Courthill Wood

Bignor Mill

Manor Farm

ROMAN VILLA (remains of)

Grevatt Wood

Stane Street ROMAN ROAD (course of)

Bignor

Hadworth Barn

Jay's Farm

42

43

Upper House

West Sussex Literary Trail

BIGNOR CP

West Burton

BURY

14

Bignortail Wood

BP

Cooke's House

West Burton

Egg Bottom Coppice

28

17

Bignor Hill

BP 51

Tumulus

Westburton Hill

Tumuli

Toby's Stone

133

13

13

Tumuli

186

Tumulus

175

179

166

King's Buildings

178

Barkhale Wood

Tumulus

Tumulus

174

Bury Hill

Cross

BSs

BS

BS

Tumulus

BS

A

Bdy

12

BS

146

The Denture

Langham Buildings

129

124

Wapelgate Corner

Langham Wood

Trot Row

Houghton Forest

The Mill Ball

HO

A 29

BS

86

99

00

Cross Dyke

Contours are given in metres
The vertical interval is 5m

and then dipping gently to the National Trust car park. As you descend there are beechwoods blocking your view northwards. To the south lies the Neolithic camp of Barkhale **52** and you can also see the grassy mounds of tumuli. The track levels off just before you pass a large yew tree.

The large 'Latin' signpost hints at the presence of a nearby Roman road, and beyond a clump of yews you come to the raised embankment or 'agger' of Stane Street **53**. Walkers turn south-west on to this Roman road, which was constructed to connect Chichester with London (riders and cyclists take the parallel Roman track below). Along it would have passed corn from the Downs, iron from the Weald and trade goods imported from the Continent. At a fingerpost turn westwards off the Roman road. Nearby the National Trust have established a camping barn at Gumber Farm, where you will also find a campsite and toilets open to the public.

*Venus and the Gladiator - one of the magnificent mosaics at Bignor Roman Villa.*

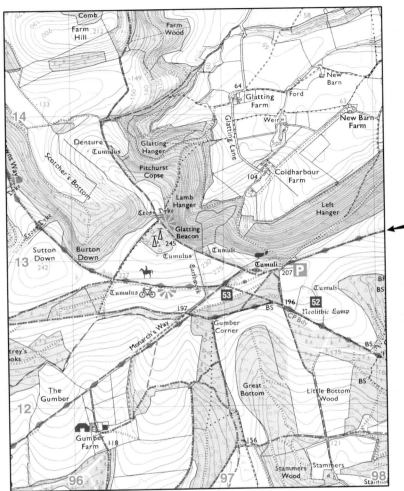

Contours are given in metres
The vertical interval is 5m

The trail is now a broad farm track with woodland to the south and grass fields to the north and the two radio masts dominating the landscape. You hardly notice the earthworks marked on the map, but pass through a wooden bridgegate next to a farm gate on their line. To the south-west you can see Chichester Cathedral and the sea

beyond. On the western side of the field pass through a hunt gate and, at a multiple bridleway junction, a signpost points you north-westwards. You follow the edge of the beech, ash and yew woodland of Burton Down. The Way cuts across the pronounced raised bank of Cross Dyke above Scotcher's Bottom. Descend gently along a broad, sometimes muddy

Goodwood Race Course

Contours are given in
The vertical interval

track from Sutton Down towards Littleton Farm and the A285.

To the north-west the battered clump of Bishop's Ring **54** stands out above the woodland of Woolavington Down. Notice the variety of trees alongside your route as the Way begins to drop steeply towards the main road. This is a dry, chalky track in summer, but in winter can become a slippery mire. Thankfully a raised walkway has been constructed near the farm.

At the road junction you go north about 20 yards before turning north-west again

at a signpost. The Way skirts Littleton Farm, then at the junction of a number of farm tracks passes through two bridlegates. Climb steeply up to Littleton Down. This is one of the few places where the Way is regularly ploughed, so be prepared for some rough going. After passing through two more bridlegates, the Way levels off and continues north-westwards through a group of woods. Nearby is Crown Tegleaze **55**, at 830 feet (253 metres) one of the highest points on the Sussex Downs.

After about 330 yards (300 metres) you leave the woodland and come to a multiple junction with the new Tegleaze signpost **56** erected by the Cowdray Hunt. The views to the north and west are stunning. Continue to the cross dyke where a number of paths meet and just before a second dyke you cross a byway. The route runs on the farm tracks to the north of the tree belt. Don't follow the vehicle tracks and avoid turning south to Tegleaze Farm. At Graffham Down there is an oak fingerpost **57** erected by the Society of Sussex Downsmen (now the South Downs Society) to commemorate one of their more dynamic members, Edmund Barkworth and his wife.

*Walkers on the South Downs Way overlooking Graffham Down.*

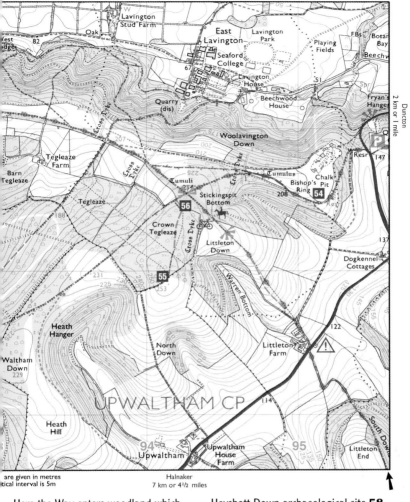

are given in metres
tical interval is 5m

Halnaker
7 km or 4½ miles

Here the Way enters woodland which gives the trail a very different character. Large clearings along Graffham Down are managed by the Graffham Down Trust to protect chalk grassland plants and butterflies.

As you come close to a forestry track called Broad Walk, a signpost indicates the Way ahead and there is a kink in the route. Head over the new cattle grid towards a series of cross dykes.

Heyshott Down archaeological site **58**, managed by the Murray Trust, contains a group of Bronze Age burial mounds dating from about 1500 BC, which mark the sites of cremations placed in pottery vessels.

The Way curves briefly southwards and then, after another cattle grid, westwards again alongside arable fields just off the top of the scarp slope on the northern edge of the woodland.

*The shadows cast by the sun highlight the terracettes on the slopes of the Downs.*

Pass south of a trig. point in the middle of a large field. To the west you can see what appears to be a forestry lookout tower, in fact a raised platform for shooting deer. You will notice a few of these peculiar contraptions. They were constructed by the Cowdray Estate as a venture to supplement the farm's income. Near the shooting tower on top of the small reservoir there are views westwards towards Cocking Down and north to the Weald. Note the traditionally layed hedge alongside your route.

At the most westerly cross dyke **59** on Heyshott Down the Way kinks and passes through this historic boundary feature. From this point the track dries out as you descend towards Cocking Hill

— a fast downhill run for mountain bikers. At Manorfarm Down the Way parts company with the woodland.

To the south of Hill Barn there is a huge timberyard full of seasoning wood, and cottages whose bright-yellow paintwork indicates that they belong to the Cowdray Estate. One is tile-hung with 'clunch' walls. This is an unusual material to see on the Downs, but is the local stone in the scarp-foot villages.

Nearby is a waterpoint — sometimes turned off in winter. The farm shop, open Friday, Saturday and Sunday, 11 am–4 pm, sells ice cream.

Continue down Hillbarn Lane to the A286, where there is a small car park opposite. If you wish to visit the fascinating collection of reconstructed medieval Weald and Downland buildings, turn south 2½ miles (3.9 km) to Singleton.

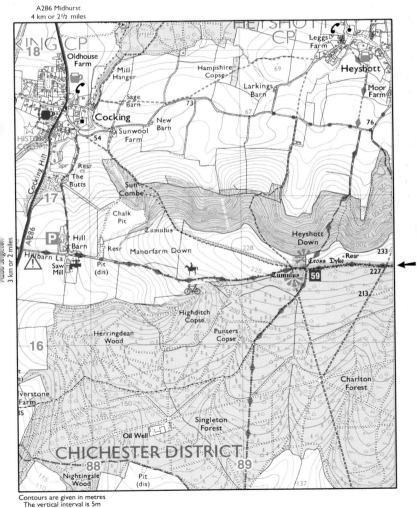

Contours are given in metres
The vertical interval is 5m

# A circular walk on Slindon Estate

*2¾ miles (4.4 km)*

This walk starts at Bignor Hill car park and has been laid out by the National Trust, who have owned and managed the area since the 1950s.

The route is marked with white waymarking and takes you south-west down Stane Street **53**, and beyond the route of the South Downs Way, to the highest point on Stane Street (646 feet/197 metres). This was probably used by the Romans as a major survey point. The raised 'agger' on the Roman road was reserved for official messengers and army manoeuvres; other people used the lower 'slow lane'.

The land marked as The Gumber on the map was once a rabbit warren. During the Second World War it was a 'dummy' airfield to deflect bombing raids from the real bases at Tangmere and Ford.

Continue down the Roman road for about 500 yards (450 metres) and then turn south to Gumber Farm. Work your way back to Gumber Corner, following the path. The woods that you pass are another example of the damage caused by the storm of 1987. The National Trust has left the majority of the wind-blown trees to act as a food source for wood-eating insects and the other wildlife that lives on them. Fortunately, new trees have begun to recolonise the area. To the north, a plantation of Scots pine acting as a 'nurse' against the wind has been thinned out, leaving a mature beech woodland.

From Gumber Corner return to the car park, or make a detour to Barkhale Neolithic camp **52**. This has been plough-damaged in the past and is one of the largest causewayed enclosures ever discovered. It has 13 separate entrances and was probably used as a tribal meeting place, where stock was slaughtered for the winter and religious and social festivals were held.

*View over the Slindon Estate.*

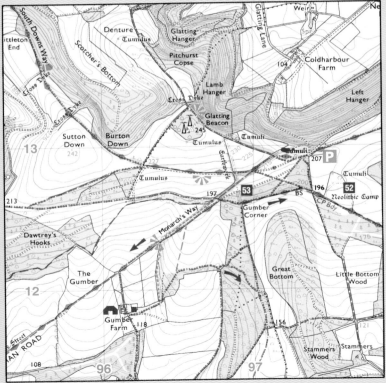

Sutton
2 km or 1 mile

Contours are given in metres
The vertical interval is 5m

# 9 Cocking to Buriton

*passing the Devil's Jumps and Harting Downs*
*11 miles (17.9 km)*

**Ascent** 1,670 feet (500 metres)
**Descent** 1,580 feet (474 metres)
**Highest point** Linch Ball: 780 feet (235 metres)
**Lowest point** Hill Top: 335 feet (100 metres)

From the car park on the A286, head westwards up Middlefield Lane. Once through Cockinghill Farm the path climbs gently towards Cocking Down between machine-trimmed hedgerows, and becomes a sunken track cut deeply into the chalk by years of use. Continue past a couple of farm tracks and an Andy Goldsworthy 'Chalk Stone' sculpture. As you gain height the hedges disappear. This is a good place to spot red kites. To the south you can see the grandstand of Goodwood racecourse and the two radio masts of the Trundle.

Cocking to Buriton

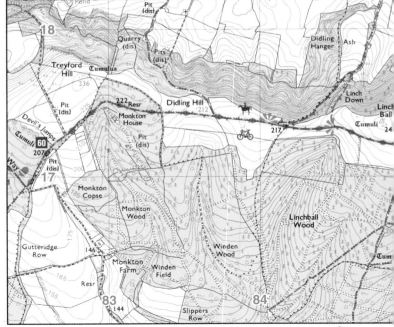

Kingley Vale Nature Reserve

Contours are given
The vertical inter

The Way runs level along the top of the Downs. The views are primarily to the south-west over the woodlands. There are grass fields either side, with no view to the north, as you are just off the scarp slope.

Just before reaching the ploughed-out cross dyke you can see the spire of Chichester Cathedral to the south-east. Beyond the dyke, there is a small line of beech trees alongside a bridleway, leading south to Kingley Vale Nature Reserve, famous for its ancient yew woodland. You pass a crude wooden ladder leading to another deer-shooting platform.

The landscape here is plateau-like and the Way descends very gently from Linch Ball to Treyford Hill. There are mole hills on the verges, but even these are full of chalk rubble, which shows how shallow the soil is here. The woodland of Didling Hanger

reaches right up to the South Downs Way. Just beyond, there are good views to the north. The trail becomes a rutted, grassy track, enclosed by sheep fences.

West of Didling Hill the route enters woods above Monkton House with a chain-link boundary fence. The Way can be muddy here because of overshading. It curves to the south-west, passing a bracken glade. Oddly, the highest fire-risk period is in winter, when the fronds are dry. About 100 yards south-west of a signpost, you can see the grassy mounds of the Devil's Jumps tumuli **60**, a spectacular group of large Bronze Age grave mounds. For a closer view, leave the route by a signposted little path.

About 550 yards (500 metres) south-west of the Devil's Jumps **60**, turn north-westwards along a broad track through

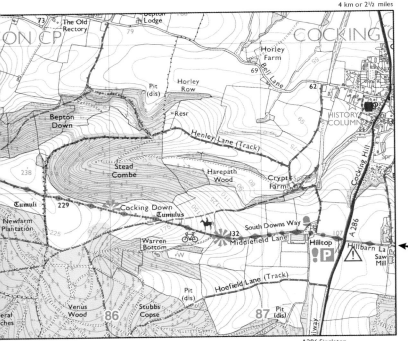

urs are given in metres
vertical interval is 5m

the woodland, where new trees have been planted. You pass a tiny memorial **61** to Hauptman Joseph Oesterman, a German pilot killed during the Second World War.

At the high point in Philliswood Down you can see westwards to Telegraph House **62**, which commemorates the sending of semaphore messages via this hill during the Napoleonic Wars. To the north and west you can see the features of Pen Hill and Beacon Hill beyond Buriton Farm.

You descend a broad chalky and, in places, very wet track to a kink in the Way above Buriton Farm and pass through your first bridlegate of the day. From here go north-westwards between barbed-wire fences on a well-trodden grassy track. There is an open feeling here with some views to the north over the Weald. The trail just touches the woodland above Rook Clift. This is a narrow, and occasionally rather muddy, section as you wind around the head of a valley.

*Looking down over the South Downs Way from Beacon Hill towards Meonstoke.*

Go round the pathway just inside Elsted Hanger. At Mount Sinai, about 100 yards before a byway crossing, a fingerpost and waymark post direct you westwards to Pen Hill up a steep, broad track, a little distance from the woodland. As you rise there are fine views, particularly eastwards along the scarp slope. This is a good riding surface, as it is softer than some of the other tracks. The Way then curves down to a cross dyke. Beyond this the Way rises gently and curves southwards, towards Telegraph House **62**, taking a long route around Beacon Hill. Although this is less difficult than going directly west, it is still quite a climb at first.

Continue south along the contours of Beacon Hill, and just touch the outer ramparts of its Iron Age fort **63**. About 30 yards into some woodland you come to a South Downs Way fingerpost directing you north-west.

In winter you will see the beautiful orange-red berries of climbing bryony among the thorn trees. As you head back around the west side of Beacon Hill you might put up a flock of pigeons or a buzzard from the woodland. To the south-west you can usually just make out the water of Chichester Harbour.

After passing through a bridlegate, drop gently into Bramshott Bottom, where you may encounter temporary gates in electric fencing used to control grazing sheep. At the head of this dry valley, the Way suddenly turns west again and there is a splendid waymark post here. Climb steeply up a broad track to the top of Harting Downs. This northern route is not marked as a right-of-way on the map but is on public access land and offers the best views, with no gates. You

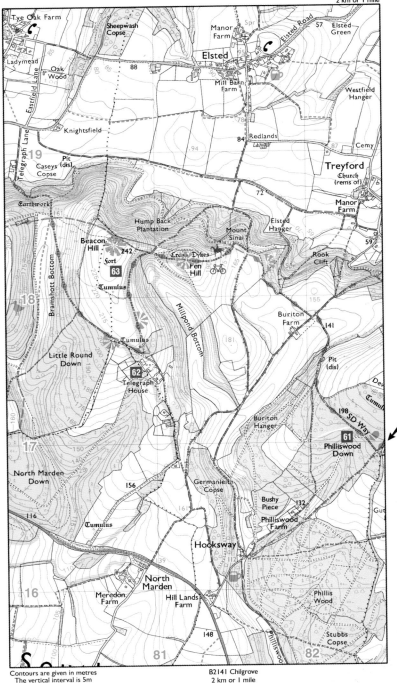

Tye Oak Farm
Sheepwash Copse
Manor Farm
Elsted Road
57
Elsted Green
Elsted
Ladymead
Oak Wood
Eastfield Lane
Telegraph Lane
88
Mill Barn Farm
Westfield Hanger
Knightsfield
78
84
Redlands
Cemy
Treyford
19
Pit (dis)
Caseys Copse
94
72
Church (rems of)
Manor Farm
Earthwork
161
Hump Back Plantation
Elsted Hanger
59
Beacon Hill
142
Mount Sinai
Cross Dykes
Rook Clift
Bramshott Bottom
Fort
63
Fen Hill
155
Tumulus
Millpond Bottom
181
Buriton Farm
141
18
Tumulus
Pit (dis)
Little Round Down
Telegraph House
62
Dev
Tumul
198 SD Way
Buriton Hanger
61
17
North Marden Down
156
Germanleith Copse
Philliswood Down
119
116
Bushy Piece
132
Tumulus
Philliswood Farm
Gut
16
Hooksway
Meredon Farm
North Marden
Hill Lands Farm
139
Phillis Wood
Stubbs Copse
148
Philliswoo
S
81
82

Contours are given in metres
The vertical interval is 5m

B2141 Chilgrove
2 km or 1 mile

can now see the spire of South Harting Church **64** in the village at the foot of the Downs. To the west there is a radio mast on top of Butser Hill. The cross dykes, where the track from Whitcombe Bottom meets the Way, are visible.

Looking west from a small clump of cankered ash, you can see the car park at Harting Hill and the ruined 18th-century banqueting room **65** on Tower Hill. Go gently down a flinty track and through a wooden bridlegate, then across the field north of the car park. Wind through a very short, narrow wooded section of the trail before you meet the busy B2141 road – cross carefully. On the far side go north-west on a narrow, sandy track, through woodland.

The Way levels out to meet the B2146. To the south lies Up Park (commonly spelt Uppark), a 1690s country house now owned by the National Trust and rebuilt after a fire in 1989. After again carefully crossing a road, you go westwards along a broad, flinty farm track called 'Forty Acre Lane'. From here it is a 2-mile (3-km), almost level, and occasionally muddy, run to the West Sussex–Hampshire boundary at Hundred Acres. The views are primarily to the north to Torberry Hill **66** and South Harting. The most dominant landscape feature is the forestry plantation of West Harting Down. You cross the tarmac of the Sussex Border Path just north of Foxcombe Farm.

B2146 Petersfield
5 km or 3 miles

Contours are given
The vertical interv

From the top of the hill at Hundred Acres descend gently towards Sunwood Farm. The unmarked county boundary **67** was the official end of the South Downs Way until it was extended to Winchester in 1989. Go south, then west through the farm. The trail rises towards The Miscombe on a road beside a line of beech trees. Watch for farm traffic.

Just before North Lodge the road turns south towards Ditcham Park School. Take a fork going westwards towards Coulters Dean Farm. Your route goes steeply down through the woods. At a sharp bend there is a signpost saying 'Public Byway' (marked on the map as 'Milky Way'). Here you curve south-west, then west past the Coulters Dean Nature Reserve to Coulters Dean Farm. Leave the tarmac and pass beneath a power line. To

*An interior of Uppark House, lovingly restored by the National Trust after the fire in 1989.*

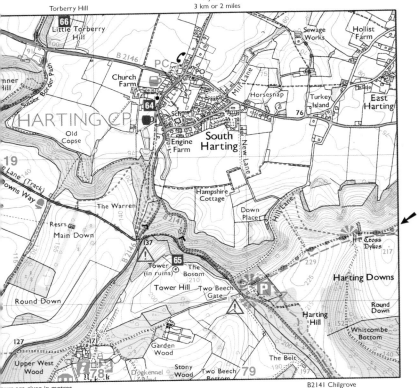

ours are given in metres
vertical interval is 5m

B2141 Chilgrove
5 km or 3 miles

the south you can see the woodland of Oakham and to the north there are good views over the Weald. At the high point above Coulters Dean Farm, you can see a quarry at Fagg's Farm, the woodland of Ludgersham Copse and Head Down Plantation ahead to the west.

The Way undulates towards Dean Barn and has a much improved new surface of fine flint pebbles. You go through the woodland of Appleton's Copse and descend steeply to New Barn Lane, along a sunken road lined with hazel, ash and old man's beard. Opposite is parking for Queen Elizabeth Country Park **68**. From

here you can go down Kiln Lane or the Hangers Way (off-road) into Buriton.

Queen Elizabeth Country Park is renowned for its downland National Nature Reserve and forest scenery. The Park Centre and café are open all year round except Christmas. You can usually purchase organic lamb, venison and wild rabbit from the park shop, as well as gifts and maps.

The Butser Hill café is open at weekends and during school holidays. WCs at Butser Hill and the Park Centre are open year round. During opening hours the visitor centre staff are happy to fill up water bottles.

# The 'blues' – a rather special group of butterflies

As you walk the Way you should spot some of the butterflies from the 'blue' family. These include the adonis, chalkhill, small, common, and holly blues, while oddly enough the brown argus is also included in the group. Two (the chalk hill and adonis) are particularly characteristic downland insects, which need the food plant horseshoe vetch and short, sheep-grazed turf.

*Adonis blue*

Surprisingly, they have developed a mutually beneficial relationship with the yellow meadow ant. The butterfly larvae and pupae are protected by the ants. In return they produce a honey-like secretion which the ants love. A case of Darwinian 'you scratch my back and I'll scratch yours!'

The hot south-facing slopes of the Downs are one of the few habitats in Britain warm enough to support the adonis blue, while you are more likely to see the holly blue on wooded downland in West Sussex. It is a real joy to discover these subtle, unpretentious, but superbly beautiful insects as you journey between Eastbourne and Winchester.

*Chalkhill blue*

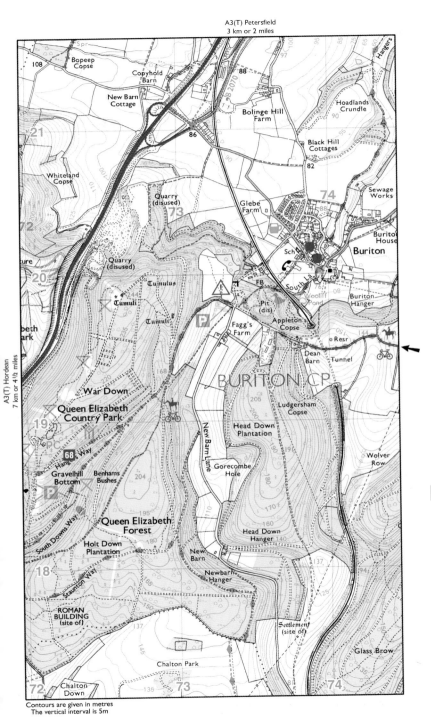

Bopeep Copse

108

Copyhold Barn

New Barn Cottage

88

86

21

Bolinge Hill Farm

Hoadlands Crundle

90

Black Hill Cottages

82

Whiteland Copse

74

Sewage Works

Quarry (disused)

73

Glebe Farm

Buriton House

Buriton

72

Quarry (disused)

Sch

South La.

Wolliff Pond

Buriton Hanger

20

Tumulus

FB

Pit (dis)

Buriton Hanger

Tumuli

Fagg's Farm

Appleton's Copse

P

Tumuli

o Resr

eth ark

War Down

Dean Barn

Tunnel

BURITON CP

Queen Elizabeth Country Park

New Barn Lane

Head Down Plantation

Ludgersham Copse

19

PC

Hang Way

68

Wolver Row

Gravelhill Bottom

Benhams Bushes

Gorecombe Hole

Queen Elizabeth Forest

P

Head Down Hanger

South Downs Way

Holt Down Plantation

New Barn

Newbarn Hanger

18

Staunton Way

ROMAN BUILDING (site of)

Settlement (site of)

Glass Brow

Chalton Park

72

Chalton Down

73

74

Contours are given in metres
The vertical interval is 5m

# 10 Buriton to Exton

*via Butser Hill and Old Winchester Hill*
*12½ miles (20.1 km)*

**Ascent** 1,300 feet (390 metres)
**Descent** 1,545 feet (460 metres)
**Highest point** Butser Hill: 815 feet (245 metres)
**Lowest point** Exton village: 200 feet (90 metres)

The route from here to Winchester will eventually be a continuous bridleway, but some sections have still to be confirmed. Although the entire highlighted route is open to walkers, riders sometimes have to use alternatives. Waymarks will indicate future changes in proposed route alignment or status.

From the western end of the Queen Elizabeth Country Park car park near Buriton, go through a gap and follow a broad gravel track rising and curving south-westwards. The path levels off overlooking Fagg's Farm.

Just past a post, with a blue South Downs Way waymarker, you come to a fork in the track. An alternative cycling and riding trail lies straight ahead, but the actual South Downs Way drops to the south-west down Gravelhill Bottom – they meet again at the bottom of the hill. Descend gently through the woodland to a clearing, equipped for picnics and barbecues. After a mile (1.6 km) there is another clearing, called Benhams Bushes. Here the metalled forest road forms a huge arc and there is another car park and picnic site. The trail goes south-west across a grassy track, and downhill,

taking the route of the Hanger's Way parallel to the park road.

At the bottom of the hill there are lots of signs relating to the Country Park **68** (see page 122) and numerous tracks leading off the internal park road – it is all very confusing. There is a horse-box park here. Head north on split trails for about 275 yards (250 metres) to the Park Centre. Horses are welcome at the Centre, but the bridleway passes just east in the woodland. There are a café, toilets and a shop here.

On leaving the Centre, go east to the rear of the building and rejoin the park paths. Head north, passing under the main road, where after about 30 yards you come to the end of a wooden railing and cross the tarmac and a gravel car park.

Northwards, you should follow the bridleway signs. You can see the climb ahead. Drop to a bridlegate, past a sign advising mountain bikes to keep to the trail.

The pasture is ideal for riding horses, but very steep. You pass through a Bronze/Iron Age field system **69**. About half a mile (0.8 km) up Butser Hill go through a bridlegate with a stile next to it.

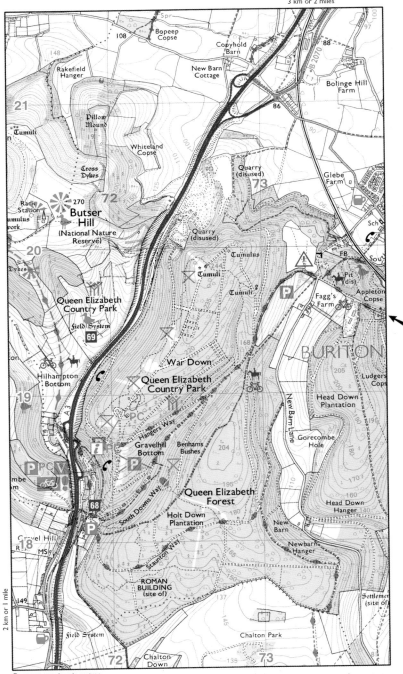

Spr

Bopeep
Copse

108

Copyhold
Barn

New Barn
Cottage

88

B 2070

Bolinge Hill
Farm

148

Rakefield
Hanger

21

86

Pillow
Mound

Tumuli

Whiteland
Copse

Quarry
(disused)

73

Glebe
Farm

Cross
Dykes

72

Sch

Radio
Station

270

Butser
Hill
(National Nature
Reserve)

Quarry
(disused)

Quarry
(disused)

Sou

20

Tumuli

FB

Pit
(dis)

Dykes

Tumuli

P

Appleton
Copse

Queen Elizabeth
Country Park

Tumuli

Fagg's
Farm

Field System

69

BURITON

205

War Down

Ludgers
Cops

19

Hilhampton
Bottom

A3

Queen Elizabeth
Country Park

Head Down
Plantation

New Barn Lane

Gorecombe
Hole

PC

Hangers Way

Gravelhill
Bottom

Benhams
Bushes

204

P

Queen Elizabeth
Forest

Head Down
Hanger

P

PC

68

South Downs Way

Holt Down
Plantation

New
Barn

Newbarn
Hanger

18

Gravel Hill

MS

Staunton Way

ROMAN
BUILDING
(site of)

Chalton Park

Settlement
(site of)

149

Field System

72

Chalton
Down

73

Contours are given in metres
The vertical interval is 10m

The whole of this hillside is used occasionally for sports such as hang-gliding, paragliding and model-glider flying, and can be a colourful, busy place. By contrast, it is also an excellent spot for downland flowers and insects. Go west of the radio masts through another narrow bridlegate. Curve around in a great arc and head towards Limekiln Lane. The number of cross dykes and Bronze Age tumuli suggest that this was a strategic site. It is worth deviating to the trig. point, near the masts, from where you can get panoramic views northwards.

Near the top of Butser Hill a mock Iron Age roundhouse forms a café with toilets and information boards. The café is only open weekends and school holidays, but there is a car park and picnic site. Unfortunately the water from the taps in the toilets is *not potable*.

The Way passes through a grass and bramble section just before it hits Limekiln Lane and leaves the Country Park. The route runs parallel to the road

on the verge side, but about 100 yards from the car park you cross over the highway and run parallel on the east side for about half a mile (0.8 km).

Butser Hill is the end of the dramatic section of the South Downs, and westwards the chalk forms a rolling plateau. Looking east, you can see the fire breaks of Queen Elizabeth Forest running straight up and down the hillside. To the west are two radio masts on Wether Down, near Mercury Park, formerly the HMS *Mercury* naval base. You come to a multiple road junction and the Way turns due west along a lane towards Tegdown Hill. You now have about 1 ¼ miles (2 km) of almost level journey to Hyden Cross.

Past a clump of four monkey-puzzle trees next to Homelands Farm the road deteriorates into a gravel track and there are high hedges of laurel, holly, beech and thorn. Continue westwards under the electricity line, with expansive views to the north. At low points on Tegdown Hill, the Way can be muddy and wet.

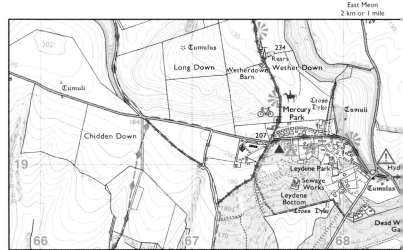

East Meon
2 km or 1 mile

Contours are given in
The vertical interval

*Hampshire countryside spread out below Butser Hill.*

From this ridge you can see the church at East Meon and the river valley below. The grassy ruts to the north show that this has been a thoroughfare for many centuries. As you enter Hyden Wood, it feels like a pretty woodland walk, but in winter trees may fall across the Way and the going can be very wet. As you descend the track gets a little drier, and there is a sheltered spot in which to sit and eat your lunch.

The Way goes past a black and white thatched cottage up the Droxford road to a junction about 100 yards ahead. Riders and pedestrians take care. Go straight across the second junction. Head north-west, parallel to the road. After about 100 yards the trail curves sharply around to head west past the Sustainability Centre, with its hostel, campsite and café. Where the road meets another junction, go north past a Cellnet aerial onto a gravelly track that rises gently towards two radio masts at the high point at Wether Down. After passing a metal barrier, you are back in open rolling downland with superb views in most directions.

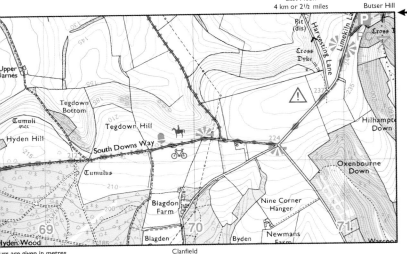

*The South Downs Way near the hamlet of Coombe Cross, looking towards Hen Wood.*

*The Downs are a huge aquifer, their water issuing from springs at their foot to create chalk streams like the one that runs through the village of East Meon.*

Beyond Wetherdown Barn, towards Salt Hill, the trail can be very muddy and slippery. The Way drops steeply off Salt Hill to the small hamlet of Coombe Cross. The trail is flinty very here, so riders should be careful. Down the slope the lane becomes a hard, sunken track. About 550 yards (500 metres) south of Coombe Cross the Way levels out and can be muddy in winter. Continue northwards, across the metalled road, and back onto the byway.

About 275 yards (250 metres) north of Coombe Cross the track kinks. It is dry even though enclosed by trees. The Way descends gently towards Henwood Down. At a dip you reach a signpost and turn west on the bridleway along a grassy headland. Mountain bikers coming down from Coombe Cross should be careful of deep ruts as they approach this turning.

Head west as the ground rises over the slopes of Henwood Down, with Hen Wood to the north. To the south you can see the

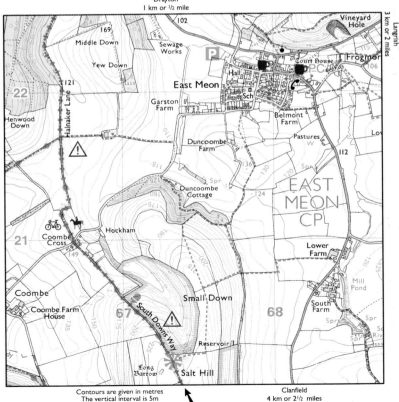

Langrish
3 km or 2 miles

Vineyard
Hole

169
Middle Down
Sewage
Works
102

Yew Down

P

Court House
Frogmor
106

22
121
East Meon
Hall
Sch

Halnaker Lane

Henwood
Down

Garston
Farm

Belmont
Farm

Duncoombe
Farm

Pastures

Lo

112

Duncoombe
Cottage

EAST
MEON
CP

115

136
130
120
124

Hockham

21
Coombe
Cross

149

Lower
Farm

Small Down

Coombe

Coombe Farm
House

67

South Downs Way

68

Mill
Pond

South
Farm

135

150
175
200

Reservoir

Long
Barrow

Salt Hill

Contours are given in metres
The vertical interval is 5m

Clanfield
4 km or 2½ miles

At the pit, take the route north-west through a pair of boxed bridlegates, diagonally up the hill towards the road. At the top by the roadside you come to another metal gate, a wooden hunt gate and a fingerpost. Where practicable, all trail-users should go south-east along the vergeside bridleway to the woodland, where you cross the road carefully and go through a signposted gap into Old Winchester Hill National Nature Reserve **71**.

The Way now continues south, running parallel to the road on the edge of the reserve. Old Winchester Hill is surmounted by an Iron Age fort **72**, whose defensive earthworks, probably from dating the 2nd century BC, may have been a tribal centre for the region east of the Meon River. The reserve is maintained by sheep grazing, so be sure to keep your dog on a lead. The nature trail parallel to the bridleway offers the best views. At the point where the main reserve access track meets the bridleway there is a 'welcome' sign. Pedestrians wishing to see the fort can use the 'easy going' trail, while horses and cyclists should use the parallel track. The South Downs Way winds around the southern edge of the reserve; overall it is level, but the surface can be muddy in winter due to heavy use. As the trail curves westwards you will see the spectacular ramparts of the Iron Age fort **72** ahead.

The bridleway route turns south and runs around the outer edge of the reserve in the adjoining fields. Pedestrians may visit the ancient monument by going through the swing gate and walking 50 yards, going west

radio masts on Wether Down. Whitewool Farm **70** and Whitewool Hanger lie to the west below Old Winchester Hill **71**. Pass alongside a metal fencepost where the bridleway becomes a concrete farm track.

On reaching the minor road, turn north-westwards by Hall Cottages. Follow the signpost to Whitewool Farm **70** past the concrete farm driveway and a little further on the asbestos barn with the big, galvanised feed hoppers. Turn south-west at a signpost and sign saying 'Meon Springs Fly Fishery' and carry on down the track past the fishery's coffee shop/bar and over a stock pond full of fat trout. The driveway curves around the main farm, goes southwards briefly and then, after passing through a triangular metal gate, turns west towards Old Winchester Hill **71**. There is a chalk pit ahead, cut into the hillside.

to cross the Iron Age fort. On a clear day you can see the Isle of Wight and Chichester Harbour.

Following three lengthy public inquiries a permanent route across the Meon Valley has been finalised; however further legal steps are required before this permanent route can be installed and opened for use. For further up-to-date information regarding progress of the route across the Meon Valley, contact the National Trail Officer via email at sdw@southdowns.gov.uk or phone 077181 46953. Write to the South Downs Way Officer, c/o Stanmer Offices, Stanmer Park, Lewes Road, Brighton BN1 9SE.

If you have chosen to visit the hill fort, the path now drops steeply to a kissing-gate and a small woodland. At the edge of the trees you come to a hunt gate and the edge of the NNR. After the end of a sheep fence is a signpost signalling different trails (Monarchs Way and South Downs Way).

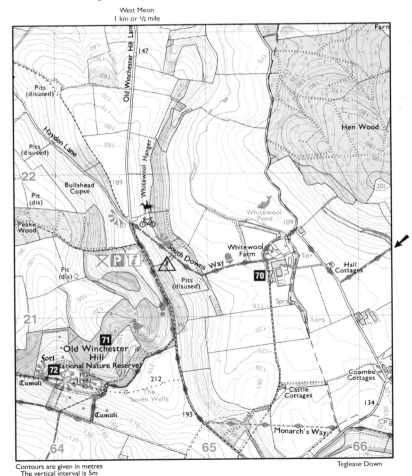

West Meon
1 km or 1/2 mile

Contours are given in metres
The vertical interval is 5m

Teglease Down

*A little egret fishes in the River Meon.*

A signpost indicates that you have rejoined the main National Trail route that skirts south of Old Winchester Hill. The path is now a broad grass track with arable fields and a hedge on the south side. The trail rises westwards with a sheep fence and grass on the north side. After about a quarter of a mile, the route gently zig-zags down to the valley floor of the River Meon. There are excellent views across to Beacon Hill National Nature Reserve, but take care to avoid falling into deep badger holes!

Just before the old railway line **73** is a badger sett inside a small wooden fence. At a metal field gate the Way does a U-turn and crosses a bridge over a winter-flowing chalk stream. It then goes up a ramp and steps to cross the old railway line.

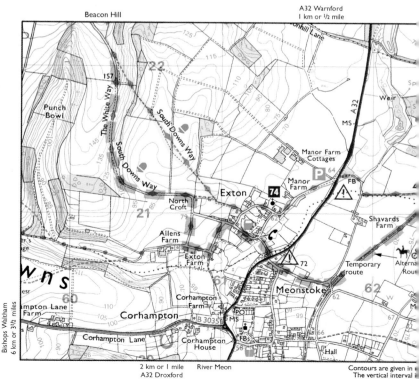

Bishops Waltham
6 km or 3½ miles

Here is the start of the temporary route for riders and cyclists – see pink dotted line on map – until a permanent route is finally resolved. Horses and cyclists (and walkers in very wet conditions) should turn south-west down the old railway line then follow the temporary route signpost along minor roads (take care when crossing the A32) until they rejoin the footpath section almost at the top of the White Way near Beacon Hill.

If taking the walkers' route from the disused railway line, turn west down a short flight of steps following the riverbank path. After a three-sleeper bridge, the Way turns northwards. The path can be very wet as you approach the River Meon. This is a beautiful chalk stream with a footbridge just wide enough for pedestrians.

Cross the main road with care to Church Lane opposite. The Way curves westwards through Exton, going north of the pub and just south of the church **74**. Inside the church, a headstone shows the Angel of Death summoning the scholar from his books. After a 12-mile (19-km) walk through the winter mud, you may feel as if he's summoning you as well!

The villages of Corhampton and Meonstoke are just south of Exton and have an excellent village store (also a post office). The Saxon church at Corhampton is a real gem, with wonderful Early English Romanesque wall paintings. Further south, the village of Droxford has hotels, B&Bs and other facilities.

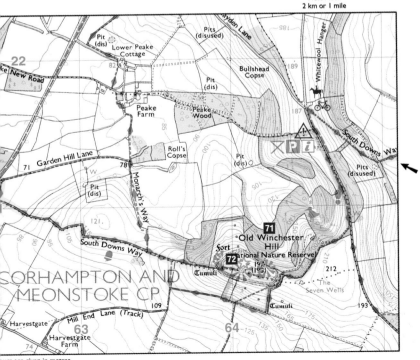

*A meadow of wild flowers at Exton.*

# ❙❙ Exton to Winchester

*through Lomer and Chilcomb*

*12 miles (19.5 km)*

**Ascent** 1,070 feet (320 metres)
**Descent** 1,170 feet (350 metres)
**Highest point** Beacon Hill (Hampshire): 665 feet (200 metres)
**Lowest point** River Itchen (Winchester): 100 feet (30 metres)

The temporary route for walkers goes westwards, past Exton Church **74**, along a curved street with a high brick and then flint wall on your south side. At a footpath sign you turn off the road to the north-west between Glebe Cottage and Bramcote House.

The route is a grassy track for 50 yards before it passes through a kissing-gate and runs along a field headland. After about 100 yards the Way turns north through a gap and then north-west again on the other side of the fence. At this kink you reach a footpath junction, where you should head north-west, avoiding the road section. The path cuts a narrow, diagonal track with many stiles/kissing-gates across a number of

*The River Meon, crossed by this bridge ne of Exton, is an attractive chalk stre*

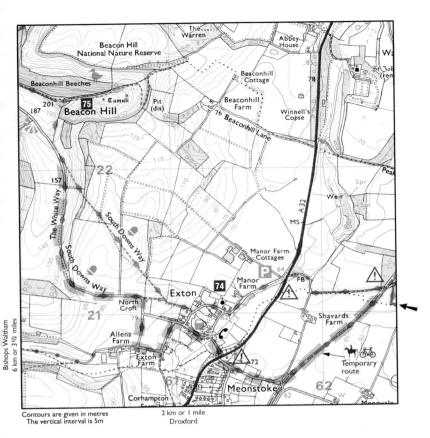

Contours are given in metres
The vertical interval is 5m

2 km or 1 mile
Droxford

arable fields and farm tracks before it passes through a tree belt and rises steeply up the south-eastern slopes of Beacon Hill.

About halfway up the hill, a magnificent view opens over the Meon Valley. As you gain height, the ash trees become stunted, and you get glimpses of Beacon Hill **75** to the north, with its nature reserve of buff-coloured chalk grassland. Just as you level off, you reach a kissing-gate and fingerpost, next to an iron field gate, where you join the metalled road and the temporary route for cyclists and horseriders. Continue uphill, and where

there is a gap between two wooden posts and a fingerpost, turn north to the trig. point on Beacon Hill and then west alongside Beaconhill Beeches until you reach a small car park.

Beacon Hill is well worth a brief diversion, particularly in spring and summer, in order to look at the typical downland flora found in this National Nature Reserve. You can see 13 species of wild orchids here, as well as round-headed rampion, kidney vetch, rock rose, horseshoe vetch and other plants. There are also Bronze Age tumuli and other early features known as 'hollow ways'.

Continue north-west on the wide road verge until, after about 275 yards (250 metres), the road turns towards the north and you carry on ahead, through a hunt gate and along a bridleway which is signposted as the South Downs Way next to a metal field gate.

Even in January, this broad, dry, flinty track provides a comfortable route for walkers and cyclists, but may be a little hard for horses.

Trees line the path as you approach Lomer Pond, with a mixture of oak, ash and beech and an understorey of blackthorn and holly. Just to the north-west of Lomer Cottage, there are humps and bumps in the field – all that remains of a lost medieval village **76**.

*Hinton Ampner house and gardens, owned by the National Trust, lie 2 miles (3 km) north of the South Downs Way and can be reached by following the Wayfarer's Walk.*

Exton to Winchester

As you approach Lomer the Way levels and is more enclosed by hedges and trees. Turn south-west for about 50 yards, then curve westwards, within the farmyard, south of two farm cottages. Once past the second cottage you turn north for about 30 yards through a locking metal hunt gate and then west again along a muddy farm track. There is an oak fingerpost here with a waymark arrow, indicating that the Wayfarer's Walk, from Emsworth in Hampshire to Inkpen Beacon near Newbury, has again joined the South Downs Way.

The trail winds westwards for half a mile (0.8 km) through a mixed arable and woodland landscape. The route is frequently used by farm vehicles and can be rather wet underfoot, but as the ground rises the going improves and becomes chalky. You can often hear the raucous call of cock pheasants in this vicinity, and there is spiky green witches'-broom to be seen in the hedge.

As you approach the road there are views over rolling downland to the north-east. You can see Hinton Ampner House in The Park near New Cheriton, and Cheriton to the north. Wind Farm **77**, which has a number of hunt gates to negotiate, is an early Victorian flint-and-brick cottage, constructed in 1803, with a mixture of tiles, slate and patterned bricks.

Follow the track and turn north through a beech copse to join the road. Cross carefully. Turn west along the path parallel to the road. There is now about 1 ¼ miles (2 km) of narrow trail, mostly beside a tree-lined verge. Watch out for exposed tree roots and remember to face oncoming traffic when you rejoin the road. Great care is required here.

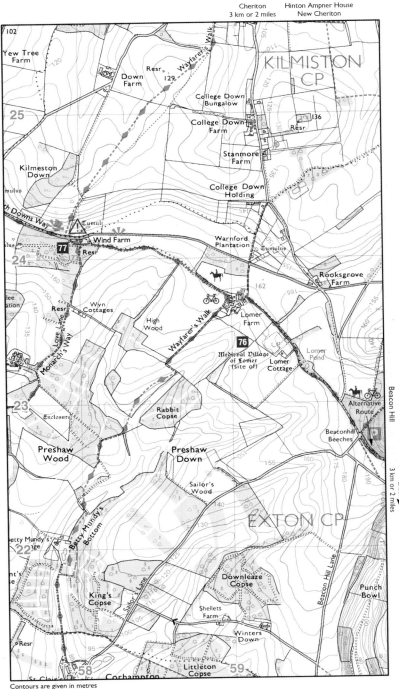

Contours are given in metres
The vertical interval is 5m

Yew Tree Farm

102

KILMISTON CP

Down Farm

Resr 129

Wayfarer's Walk

College Down Bungalow

College Down Farm

136

Resr

25

Stanmore Farm

College Down Holding

Kilmeston Down

South Downs Way

Tumuli

Warnford Plantation

Cumulus

Wind Farm

77

Resr

Rooksgrove Farm

24

162

991

Wyn Cottages

High Wood

Lomer Farm

Monarch's Way

Love Lane

Resr

Wayfarer's Walk

76

Medieval Village of Lomer (site of)

Lomer Cottage

Lomer Pond

Alternative Route

Beacon Hill

23

Enclosure

Rabbit Copse

Beaconhill Beeches

Preshaw Wood

Preshaw Down

Sailor's Wood

155

Exton
3 km or 2 miles

EXTON CP

Betty Mundy's

Betty Mundy's Bottom

King's Copse

Sailor's Lane

Downleaze Copse

Beacon Hill Lane

Punch Bowl

22

Shellets Farm

Resr

Winters Down

95

58

Corhampton

Littleton Copse

59

Just before a T-junction signposted Kilmeston, by the entrance to Preshaw House, the views north are beautiful.

Adjacent to the road junction is Mill Barrows **78** – a distinct grassy knoll. It is an ancient burial mound and the local hill top, Millbarrow Down, is named after it. About 330 yards (300 metres) west, turn north at a crossroads.

The pub shown as The Fox and Hounds on old maps has been renamed Milburys. There is a treadmill inside that used to draw water from a deep well cut in the chalk. The barmaid will tell you all sorts of fables and give you ice cubes to drop down the well. From Milburys, go north about 100 yards and then turn north-west, following the signpost towards High Stoke. From here, the Way descends north-westwards towards Holden Lane. Where the tarmac road turns north-east, continue in a northerly direction, past a Dutch barn. Holden Lane can be a little muddy in places, but is usually a level, dry farm track.

The path drops gently towards Ball's Lane and your route beyond is a broad farm track lined with beech trees among arable fields. You see the cottages on the A272 beyond Holden Farm before catching glimpses of the agricultural buildings that lie in a little dip. The iron field gates here are generally left open. Note the neat system enabling riders to open the gate.

Go through a double wooden field gate by the road, cross with great care, and carry on in a northerly direction, rising gently past the cottages. After about 275 yards (250 metres) you come to another farm gate and hunt gate. Go through the gate and go directly across the field on the licensed bridleway or east along the headland. At the easternmost corner of the field you do a U-turn and head north-west along the fenceline. The path north from this field corner is a safe route to Cheriton. North-east of Ganderdown Farm the South Downs Way becomes a sunken track. Pass through a wooden hunt gate at Ganderdown Farm.

Under the electricity lines go through a metal bridlegate alongside a field gate. The Way is bounded by two neat hedges and rises gently north-west towards a Dutch barn on the skyline. On top of Gander Down a bridleway leads north-east to Cheriton. Looking back to Ganderdown Farm, there seem to be signs of a Celtic or medieval field system. The landscape is still plateau-like.

Continue north-west from Gander Down for 275 yards (250 metres) through a metal bridlegate next to a field gate, across a road (Rodfield Lane), and under a metal barrier. Keep heading north-west along the 'King's Way' for about 1 ¼ miles (2 km) over undulating 'prairie' to

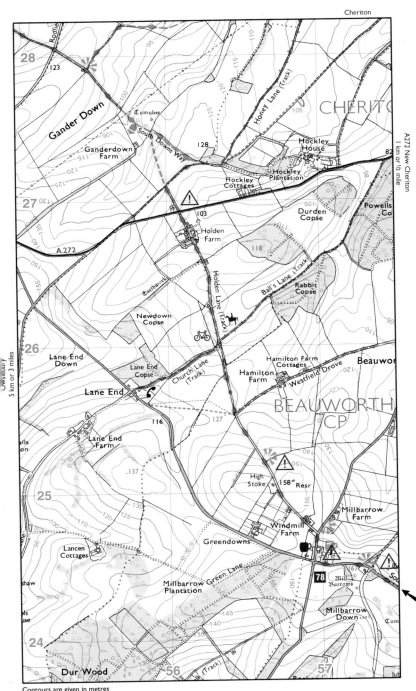

Contours are given in metres
The vertical interval is 5m

Round Clump. Just to the north, at a group of farm buildings and a cottage, change direction and head south-west. Rising towards Cheesefoot Head, the landscape becomes arable again, with groups of trees and glimpses of Winchester to the west of Chilcomb Down. Beside Great Clump the Way passes through a wooden gate and between barbed-wire fences, with a line of beech trees and a mixed woodland to the east. Then it becomes a beautiful beech archway with fine views out to the scarp slope. To the west you can see the tree-planting on Telegraph Hill **79**.

The path passes just to the north of Cheesefoot Head car park to a bridlegate near the roadside. Cross the road carefully and go through a gap next to a field gate. The Way is signposted north-west at the far edge of this narrow field, heading towards the southernmost

corner of the rectangular coniferous woodland on Telegraph Hill. The views to the south and south-west begin to open up, and you can see as far as the oil refinery at Fawley. At the tumulus near Telegraph Hill, the views over Winchester and the modernistic Intech Science Centre are spectacular. From here, turn west down towards Deacon Hill **80**. The Way is a farm track with a windbreak plantation to the south-west.

At a path junction the Way kinks south then goes south-west towards Deacon Hill **80**. At Little Golders the trail turns north-west down a sunken, metalled track, away from a flagpole and sign that warn of Army Ranges. Drop steeply north towards Hillacre Farm, past a fingerpost pointing east back up the hill as the road curves round into Chilcomb. As you enter Chilcomb, notice the old, black, tarred and tile-roofed granary sitting astride 'staddle

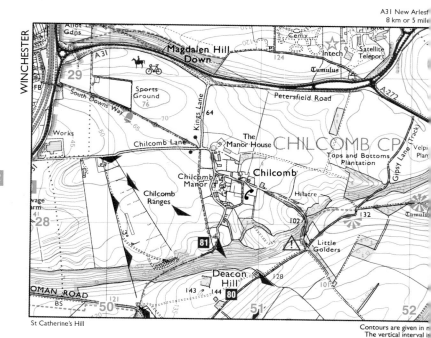

Contours are given in m
The vertical interval is

St Catherine's Hill

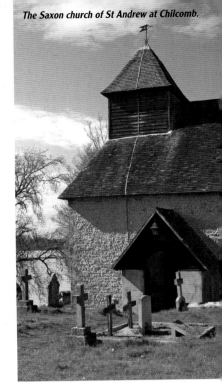

*The Saxon church of St Andrew at Chilcomb.*

stones', an ancient and effective device for keeping out the rats. There is a large brick barn at Sunshine Manor, which was once a group of three farm cottages. The road curves north at Chilcomb Manor and on to The Manor House.

At the village pond, turn west to Kings Lane, and at the junction with Chilcomb Lane go over a stile and down a headland path, beside a rabbit-proof fence, in a north-westerly direction towards Winchester. From this junction you can divert due south to Chilcomb Church **81** up a headland path. This early Saxon church is well worth a visit; it still uses a bell that was cast in 1380. The ranges are clearly visible against the hillside to the west.

Return to the junction at Kings Lane and head north-west along a footpath with Magdalen Hill Down to the north. Horseriders and cyclists currently have to leave the Way at Chilcomb and follow the diversion along Kings Lane to the A31. To the south you can see the Iron Age hill fort of St Catherine's Hill.

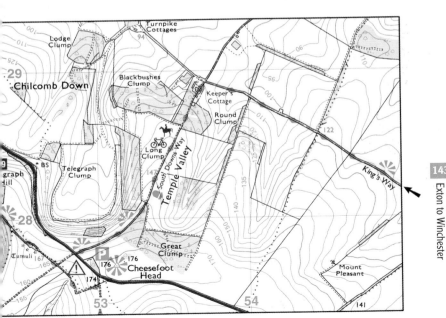

Exton to Winchester

ours are given in metres
e vertical interval is 5m

Cross the bridge over the busy M3 and at the far side turn north for 275 yards (250 metres), parallel to the motorway. At a T-junction turn west towards The Soke in Winchester.

Pass All Saints' Parish Church, a well-built, knapped flint Victorian building, and go to the junction of Canute Road and Highcliffe Road, past the 'thin' Michaelmas Cottage (1890) and then down Petersfield Road and East Hill to The Black Rat and The Blackboy pub. Cross Chesil Street at the pedestrian crossing, where the South Downs Way signs point north. However, for a more attractive route, turn south back towards Wharf Hill. Turn west down the alleyway alongside The Black Rat and past The Blackboy pub.

## King Alfred

The trail end is marked by the mighty statue of Kind Alfred the Great. Alfred (AD 849–99) is widely regarded as the first true King of England, with Winchester his capital. After defeating the Danes he ruled over all of Wessex, West Mercia and Kent.

Cross the River Itchen over a millrace footbridge at Segrim's Mill. Turn north at the walls of Wolvesey Castle and head for the High Street alongside the river. At the stone road bridge turn west into Winchester, the Saxon capital of England.

You have now completed the South Downs Way. Well done! Having travelled a hundred miles on this ancient route you can complete the experience with a final historic flourish by walking south alongside the river to the Abbey of St Cross **83**. Here, if you knock on the door of the Porter's Lodge, you will be given the 'Wayfarer's Dole'. This is a small glass of ale and a piece of bread – the oldest charity in England.

WINCHESTER

Contours are given in metres
The vertical interval is 5m

# PART THREE
# Useful Information

## Transport

The South Downs Way team produces a public transport guide annually. For details contact the National Trail Officer or visit:
- ⓘ www.nationaltrail.co.uk/southdowns
- ✉ sdw@southdowns.gov.uk

### Rail

There are regular services to major towns at the start and finish of the Way, and to other villages and towns either nearby or along the route.

You can gain access to the Way via the Eastbourne trains from London (Victoria) every half hour (hourly evening and Sundays) to Lewes, Polegate or Eastbourne (change at Lewes for Newhaven and Seaford via Southease). You can also get on and off at Plumpton, Cooksbridge, Glynde, Berwick and Southease, but as these are rural stations, the services are less frequent. (NB Many trains divide at Haywards Heath, so do ensure that you are in the correct section or you could wind up in Bognor Regis!) Regular trains also go from London (Victoria and London Bridge) to Hassocks Brighton, and there are more westerly services to Amberley and Arundel via Pulborough. There are also good services south of the Downs via Shoreham, Worthing and Chichester. Trains also run from Waterloo to Petersfield and Winchester. You may take bicycles on trains, generally free of charge. However, due to very limited space, you need to book bikes on intercity or small commuter trains (a small fee may be charged). Some services do not allow bikes at peak times, so check.

For passenger train information ring 08457 484950 or visit www.nationalrail.co.uk

## Buses

Since deregulation in October 1986, local and country bus services have been operated by a wide variety of companies. The best way to obtain comprehensive information is to call the national public-transport information service, Traveline, on ☎ 0871 200 2233 or visit
- ⓘ www.traveline.co.uk

## Baggage

Baggage-transfer facilities are available along the South Downs Way. For details and prices contact: Footprints on ☎ 01903 813381
- ⓘ www.footprintsofsussex.co.uk

See also South Downs Baggage Transfers:
- ⓘ www.southdownsbaggagetransfer.com

## Accommodation and Tourist Information Centres

Accommodation information is available (and downloadable free) from the trail website at
- ⓘ www.nationaltrail.co.uk/southdowns.

The National Trail website also has information on maps and guides, horsebox parking, drinking water taps, mountain bike hire and much more.

All the local Tourist Information Centres will help you to find accommodation (see list of addresses and telephone numbers below). Some libraries in West Sussex have certain tourist information but do not make accommodation bookings.

**Eastbourne,** East Sussex: 3 Cornfield Road, Eastbourne BN21 4QA
- ☎ 0871 663 0031 (50p/min. standard rate)
- ⓘ www.visiteastbourne.com

**Seaford,** East Sussex: 37 Church Street, Seaford BN25 1HG
- ☎ 01323 897426
- ✉ seaford.tic@lewes.gov.uk
- ⓘ www.enjoysussex.info

**Lewes**, East Sussex: 187 High Street, Lewes BN7 2DE
☎ 01273 483448
ⓘ www.lewes.gov.uk.
For a more comprehensive list of B&Bs see:
ⓘ www.lewesbandb.co.uk

**Brighton and Hove**, East Sussex: Royal Pavillion Shop, 4–5 Pavillion Buildings, Brighton BN1 1EE
☎ 0906 711 2255 (50p/min. standard rate)
ⓘ www.visitbrighton.com

**Steyning Library**, Church Street, Steyning BN44 3YB
☎ 01903 812751
(Just tourist information – no accommodation bookings, but they have a list of local B&Bs.)

**Worthing**, West Sussex: Chapel Road, Worthing BN11 1HA
☎ 01903 221066
ⓘ www.visitworthing.co.uk

**Bognor Regis**, West Sussex: Belmont Street, Bognor Regis, PO21 1BJ
☎ 01243 823140
ⓘ www.sussexbythesea.com

**Chichester, West Sussex**: 29a South Street, Chichester PO19 1AH
☎ 01243 775888
ⓘ www.visitsussex.org

**Petersfield**, Hampshire: The Library, 27 The Square, Petersfield GU32 3HH
☎ 01730 268829 (closed Thurs pm)
ⓘ www.petersfieldinfo@btconnect.com

**Winchester**, Hampshire: The Guildhall, High Street, Winchester SO23 9GH
☎ 01962 840500
ⓘ www.visitwinchester.co.uk
ⓘ www.tourism@winchester.gov.uk

A more general guide to accommodation in the Sussex area is available at
ⓘ www.visitsussex.org

For information on youth hostels and membership of the YHA, contact Youth Hostels Association, Trevelyan House, Dimple Road, Matlock, Derbyshire DE4 3YH
☎ 0800 0191 700; 01629 592700
ⓘ www.yha.org.uk.

There are youth hostels (often full – book in advance) at:

**Eastbourne**
☎ 0845 371 9316
✉ eastbourne@yha.org.uk

**Alfriston**
☎ 0845 371 9101
✉ alfriston@yha.org.uk

**Telscombe**
☎ 0845 371 9663 For reservations contact Eastbourne Youth Hostel

**Southease** may open 2012 – contact YHA headquarters for information

**Truleigh Hill**
☎ 0845 371 9047
✉ truleighhill@yha.org.uk

**Arundel**
☎ 0845 371 9002
✉ arundel@yha.org.uk

## Camping

For an up-to-date, comprehensive list of all campsites on or near the South Downs Way, go the National Trail website at
ⓘ www.nationaltrail.co.uk/southdowns

The National Trust run a camping barn/campsite at Gumber almost on the South Downs Way near Bignor.
☎ 01243 814484, or
✉ katie.archer@ nationaltrust.org.uk
An independent hostel has opened at The Sustainability Centre, Wetherdown, Droxford Road, East Meon, Hampshire GU32 1HR,
☎ 01730 823549
ⓘ www.sustainability-centre.org.uk

# Cyclists

Cyclists riding the Way have a fairly wide choice of shops that carry supplies and spares. 🚲 signifies they also do hire. Going east to west, these are:

**Evolution Cycles**, 23a Cavendish Place, Eastbourne BN21 3EJ
☎ 01323 737320
ⓘ www.evocycles.co.uk

**Phoenix Cycles**, 219 Seaside, Eastbourne
BN22 7NR
☎ 01323 729060
ⓘ www.phoenixcycles.co.uk

**The Tri Store**, 49 Grove Road, Eastbourne
BN21 4TX
☎ 01323 417071
ⓘ www.thetristore.com

**Cycleman**, 46 Rosebery Avenue, Hampden
Park, Eastbourne BN22 9QB
☎ 01323 501157

**Kontour Cycles**, 2 Millfields, Station Road,
Polegate BN26 6AS
☎ 01323 482368
ⓘ www.kontourcycles.co.uk

**Cuckmere Cycle Company**, The Barn,
Seven Sisters Country Park, Exceat, Seaford,
East Sussex BN25 4AD
☎ 01323 870310
ⓘ www.cuckmere-cycle.co.uk
NB This also has specialist hire equipment
for the disabled.

**Mr Cycles**, 26 Clinton Place, Seaford
BN25 1NP
☎ 01323 893130
ⓘ www.mrcycles.co.uk

**Halfords**, Unit C, The Drove, Newhaven
BN9 0AG
☎ 01273 515885

**Future Cycles**, 39A Friars Walk, Lewes
BN7 2LJ
☎ 01273 483108
ⓘ www.futurecycles.co.uk

**Cycles Shack**, Old Woolworth Store,
Cliffe High Street, Lewes BN7 2AN
☎ 01273 479688
ⓘ www.lewescycleshack.co.uk

**Rayment Cycles**, 13/14 Circus Parade,
New England Road, Brighton BN1 4GW
☎ 01273 697617
ⓘ www.raymentcycles.co.uk

**Planet Cycles**, West Pier, Kings Road
Promenade, Kings Road Brighton BN1 2FL
☎ 01273 748881
(open Friday–Monday from October to March,
otherwise every day except Wednesday).

**Freedom Bikes**, 45 George Street,
Brighton BN2 1RJ
☎ 01273 681698
ⓘ www.freedombikes.co.uk

**Halfords**, Unit 1, Pavilion Park, Lewes
Road, Brighton BN2 3QA
☎ 01273 604833

**Baker Street Bikes**, 7–8 York Place,
Brighton BN1 4GU
☎ 01273 675754
ⓘ www.bakerstbikes.co.uk

**Strudwick Cycles**, 28 Oxford Street,
Brighton BN1 4LA
☎ 01273 609015 (mainly repairs).

**Sydney Street Bikes**, 24 Sydney Street,
Brighton BN1 4EN
☎ 01273 624700

**Cycle Store**, 93 London Road, Brighton
BN1 4JF
☎ 01273 605160
ⓘ www.myspokes.co.uk

**Webbs Cycles**, 91 Boundary Road, Hove
BN3 7GA
☎ 01273 417658
ⓘ www.webbscycles.co.uk

**Syds Bikes 2**, 73 Portland Road, Hove
BN3 5DP
☎ 01273 747222
ⓘ www.sydsbikes2.co.uk

**Hove Cycles**, 101 Blachington Road, Hove
BN3 3YG
☎ 01273 778360
ⓘ www.hovecycles.com

**Raleigh Cycle Centre**, 38–42 Kingston
Broadway, Shoreham by Sea BN43 6TE
☎ 01273 596368
ⓘ www.mailorderbikes.com

**MSG Bikes/Lancing Cycles**,
20 Crabtree Lane, Lancing BN15 9PQ
☎ 01903 752308
ⓘ www.msgbikes.com
(made-to-measure bikes and tandem hire)

**Michael's Cycles**, 21 South Farm Road,
Worthing BN14 7AD
☎ 01903 232884

**South Downs Bikes**, 301 Goring Road, Worthing BN12 4NX
☎ 01903 244644
ⓘ www.southdownsbikes.com

**The Bike Store**, 65 Brighton Road, Worthing BN11 3EE
☎ 01903 206311
ⓘ www.thebikestore.co.uk

**Raleigh Cycle Centre**, 31 Chatsworth Road, Worthing BN11 1LY
☎ 01903 823370

**South Downs Bikes**, The Forge, 38 West Street, Storrington, West Sussex RH20 4EE
☎ 01903 745534
ⓘ www.southdownsbikes.com

**Cyclelife**, Rear of 40, Dragon Street, Petersfield GU31 4JJ
☎ 01730 266644
ⓘ www.petersfieldcycles.com

**Owens Cycles**, Stoner Hill, Steep, Petersfield GU32 1AG
☎ 01730 260446

**P. Hansford Cycles**, 91 Oliver's Battery Road South, Oliver's Battery, Winchester SO22 4JQ
☎ 01962 877555

**Halfords**, Moorside Road, Winnall, Winchester SO23 7RX
☎ 01962 849411

**Hargroves Cycles**, 10 City Road, Winchester, SO23 8SD
☎ 01962 860005
ⓘ www.hargrovescycles.co.uk

NB *To our knowledge only Halfords, Raleigh Cycle Centre, Worthing, and South Downs Bikes, Storrington, open on Sundays, but it is worth telephoning to see if this has changed.*

## Other mountain bike hire

**Meon Valley Cycle Hire**, Hants (groups only)
☎ 07778 410532
ⓘ www.meonvalley-cyclehire.co.uk

**M's Cycle Hire**, West Sussex
☎ 07852 986165
ⓘ www.m-cyclehire.co.uk

**Saddle Skedaddle** (guided and supported cycle holidays, including bike hire)
☎ 01912 651110
ⓘ www.skedaddle.co.uk

**Bike 360**, Devil's Dyke, Brighton
☎ 08466 434360
ⓘ www.bike360.co.uk

**Hassocks Community Cycle Hire,** Hassocks Hotel, Station Approach East, Hassocks, BN6 8HN
☎ 07521 961909
ⓘ www.visithassocks.co.uk

## The Mountain Bike Code

**1. Stay on Track**
Only ride on bridleways, restricted byways or byways.

**2. Respect Other Users**
Remember that on bridleways you must give way to walkers and horse riders. Make sure they can hear your approach with a friendly shout or ring of a bell and pass others slowly.

**3. Bunching Is Harassing**
If you're a large group ride in smaller groups of three or four. If the leader opens a gate be sure that the last one through knows to close it.

**4. Prevent Erosion**
Ride with control and at a speed where you can stop safely without skidding.

**5. Respect Our Ancestors**
Avoid lumps and bumps next to the Trail; these are probably ancient burial mounds or other historic sites.

**6. Follow the Countryside Code**
Remember to leave gates and property as you find them, protect plants and animals, take all your litter home and keep dogs under close control.

**7. Take Pride in Your Bike**
A well-maintained bike is a safe bike that makes your ride easier. Be sure to check brakes and tyres before you ride and take a small repair kit and spare inner tube with you.

**8. Enjoy the Ride!**
Enjoy yourself and make time to stop and take in the stunning landscape. When resting, stop to one side of the Trail to allow others to pass.

# Walking and cycling holidays

The website Walk & Cycle organises self-guided walking and cycling holidays along the South Downs Way and through the new national park, including baggage transfer, cycle hire and delivery/collection of bikes. For details see
ⓘ www.walkandcycle/southdownsway

Walkers and cyclists will also find details of accommodation, places to eat, suggested itineraries, attractions, etc., in the South Downs National Park at
ⓘ www.southdownsdiscovery.com

# Horseriders

If you damage your gear, there are a limited number of saddlers along or near the Way. Going east to west these are:

**Leonard Stevens** (Rider's Realm), 16 Crown Street, Eastbourne BN21 1NX
☎ 01323 734496 (closed Wednesdays)

**Polegate Saddlery**, 3 Millfield, Station Road, Polegate, East Sussex BN26 6AS
☎ 01323 483382 (open Saturdays, closed Thursdays and Sundays)

**The Equine Warehouse**, The Depot, Spring Gardens, Lewes, East Sussex BN7 2PT
☎ 01273 483399
ⓘ www.farmcareuk.com
(open Monday to Saturday, 9–5; can help with tack and feed)

**Dragonfly Saddlery**, The Old Goods Shed, Station Goods Yard, off Keymer Road, Hassocks BN6 8JA
☎ 01273 844606/843606
ⓘ www.dragonflysaddlery.co.uk (open all week)

**Edingtons**, 6 Onion Parade, Hassocks, West Sussex BN6 8QA
☎ 01273 844621

**Brendon Horse and Rider Centre**, London Road, Pyecombe, Nr Brighton, West Sussex BN45 7ED
☎ 01273 845545 (open Mondays to Saturdays, next to SD Way)

**Geoff Dean** (Saddlers and Harness Makers), King's Parade, 122 Findon Road, Worthing, West Sussex BN14 0AT
☎ 07854 727908
ⓘ www.geoff-dean.com
(specialises in driving harness)

**South Down Saddlery**, 2 The Square, Worthing BN14 0TE
☎ 01903 872341

**The Hack & Tack**, Foschinis Nursery, Hangleton Lane, Worthing BN12 6PP
☎ 01903 503555

**Norton Hind Saddlery**, The Parade, Arundel Road, Arundel BN18 0SD
☎ 01243 543191

**Sarah Trenchard**, 271 Holland Wood, Balls Cross Road, Petworth GU28 9JN
☎ 01798 344037

**Logo Saddlery**, 8 Bepton Road, Midhurst GU29 9LU
☎ 01730 817016

**Meadowlea Saddles**, Unit 1, Brocklands Farm, West Meon, Petersfield GU32 1JN
☎ 07979 052423

# Farriers on or near the South Downs Way (east to west)

## East Sussex

**John Henty**, 21a Lower Road, Old Town, Eastbourne, East Sussex BN21 1QE
☎ 01323 721938, mobile: 0797 6260806

**T. Goswell**, 2 Huggetts Lane, Eastbourne BN22 0LX
☎ 01323 508039

**Tony Phillips**, 3 Chartwell Close, Beacon Heights, Seaford, East Sussex BN25 2XQ
☎ 01323 890242

**C. Dean and Sons**, The Forge, Mill Lane, Rodmell, Lewes, East Sussex BN7 3HS
☎ 01273 474740, mobile: 07967 693 577

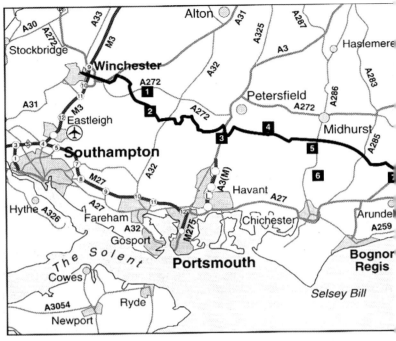

# Horsebox parking

(page references are to maps in main text)

**1 Cheesefoot Head** SU529277
Very useful car park on the A272 4 miles (6.4 km) east of Winchester (page 139).

**2 Beacon Hill Beeches** SU598228
Horses can be unboxed at the car park at the nature reserve. This site gives access to the western section of the Way (page 139).

**3 Queen Elizabeth Country Park** SU718185
There is a site for box-parking near the Park Centre at Gravel Hill car park with access to toilets and a café (page 127).

**4 Harting Down** car park SU790181
National Trust. On the B2146 1 mile (1.6 km) south of South Harting (page 123).

**5 Cocking** car park SU875166
Small car park on the A286, 1 mile (1.6 km) south of Cocking, next to the Way. Enjoyable rides to Queen Elizabeth Country Park or back to Whiteways (page 119).

**6 Goodwood Country Park** SU898113
Convenient car parks for those coming from the coastal plain, 4 miles (6.4 km) south of the Way. Parking at Harroways and Counter's Gate (south of page 113).

**7 Whiteways** car park TQ002108
At Bury Hill off the A29 roundabout. Giving access to a large bridleway network plus café and toilets (south of page 107).

**8 Washington** car park TQ120120
Off A24, 1 mile (1.6 km) south of the Washington roundabout. Good access to the east. Alternative route for riders using the Way via the village (page 97).

**9 Beeding Hill** TQ208096
High above the Adur Valley giving access to the Fulking Escarpment (page 82).

**10 High Trees** car park TQ197098
At the Upper Beeding roundabout on the A283. Ideal spot for going either east or west (page 87).

**11 Devil's Dyke** TQ259109
Popular tourist spot. Midweek parking best, busy school holidays. Good access along the Way (page 79).

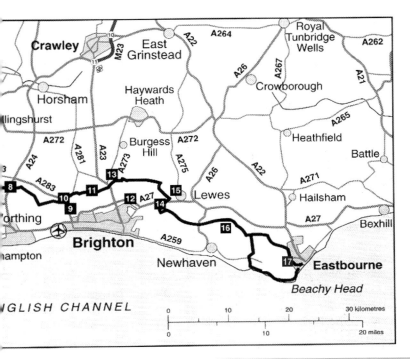

**12 Stanmer Park** TQ337096
A number of hard standings where boxes may
be parked. Several bridleways lead south to
the Woodingdean/Lewes area, and north to
the Way and the Weald (south of page 71).

**13 Jack and Jill Windmills** TQ303134
Popular and well-used box-park off the A273
with good bridleway links. Can be busy at
weekend, less so during the week (page 73).

**14 Newmarket Crossing** TQ377091
Old road lay-by. Suitable only for riders
going east as road crossing is extremely
dangerous. Access to Kingston Ridge and
Juggs Road link to Brighton (page 69).

**15 Housdean Farm** TQ368093
Old road lay-by with access to safe bridge
crossing of the A27. Suitable for both east
and west travel (page 69).

**16 Bopeep** TQ494051
Above Alciston with steep approach road
(page 56).

**17 Warren Hill** TQ588979
On B2103 near trail. Best point to start or finish
near Eastbourne. Pay & display (page 47).

*Riders on the South Downs Way.*

## West Sussex

**Ross Eager**, Manor Barn, Sands Farm, Dial Post, West Sussex RH13 8NY
☎ 07808 078498

**Kevin White**, 20 Furzeland Way, Sayers Common, Hassocks, West Sussex BN6 9JB
☎ 01273 834225, mobile: 07970 935 258

**Mark Hall**, 4 Homelands Cottages, Bines Road, Partridge Green, Horsham, West Sussex RH13 8EQ
☎ 01403 710586

**Total Foot Protection Ltd**, Bridge House Equestrian Centre, Five Oaks Road, Horsham RH13 0QW
☎ 01403 791000
ⓘ www.totalfootprotection.com

**Weller SF**, 2 Worthing Road, Dial Post, Horsham RH13 8NQ
☎ 01403 710168

**Christopher Peacock**, Wiston Forge, beside Wiston House, Steyning Road, Wiston, West Sussex BN44 3DF
☎ 01903 813445, mobile: 07850 339685

**Martin Hogan**, 2 New Cottages, Gallops Farm, Findon, Worthing, West Sussex BN14 0RQ
☎ 01903 873348, mobile: 0785 0441891

## Hampshire

**John Launder**, 2 Castle Road, Rowland's Castle, Hants PO9 6AS
☎ 02392 412645

**Mark Philips**, Coxton, Highbridge Road, Colden Common, Winchester, Hants SO21 1RW
☎ 01962 712433, mobile: 0776 7418160

**Richard Moss,** The Forge, 75 Froxfield Green, Petersfield, Hants GU32 1DQ
☎ 01730 263536, mobile: 07836 512 569

**Richard Lovejoy**, High Cross, Hill Farm Road, Monckwood, Alresford, Hants SO24 0HG. mobile: 07899 816131

**Alan and David Povey**, The Forge, Owlslebury, Winchester, Hants SO21 1LY
☎ 01962 777473

# Vets

In case your horse is injured or your dog gets sick! This list is *not* comprehensive but it covers some of the ground (east to west). If these vets cannot help, try the local Yellow Pages for more information.

**Eastbourne:** St Anne's Veterinary Group, 6 St Anne's Road, Eastbourne BN21 2DJ
☎ 01323 640011
(24-hour emergency service; horses and dogs)

**Laughton:** The Cliffe Veterinary Group, Equine Clinic, Mill Lane, Laughton BN8 6AJ
☎ 01323 815120
(24-hour emergency service; horses)

**Lewes:** The Cliffe Veterinary Group, Radstock House, 21 Cliffe High Street, Lewes BN7 2AH
☎ 01273 473232
(24-hour emergency service; dogs)

**Haywards Heath**: Cinder Hill Equine Clinic, Cinder Hill Lane, Horsted Keynes, Haywards Heath RH17 7BA
☎ 01342 811335
(24-hour emergency service; horses)

**Brighton**: The Cliffe Veterinary Group, 57 Warren Way, Woodingdean, Brighton BN2 6PH
☎ 01273 302609
(24-hour emergency service; dogs)

**Henfield:** Hawthorn Veterinary Surgeries, Wantley Cottages, London Road, Henfield, West Sussex BN5 9JP
☎ 01273 495227 or 01403 710332
(24-hour emergency service; dogs)

**Steyning:** Crossways Veterinary Group, 2 High Street, Steyning BN44 3GG
☎ 01903 816428
(24-hour emergency service; dogs)

**Horsham**: Anvil Equine Veterinary Clinic, Tuckmans Farm, Bar Lane, Copsale, Horsham RH13 9AY
☎ 01403 731213
(24-hour emergency service; horses)

**Horsham**: Mayer & Scrine Equine Veterinary Practice, Dawes Farm, Bognor Road, Warnham, Horsham RH12 3SH
☎ 01306 628222
(24-hour emergency service; horses)

**Storrington**: Crossways Veterinary Group, The Surgery, 43 School Hill, Storrington RH20 4NA
☎ 01903 743040
(24-hour emergency service; dogs)

**Arundel**: The Equine Veterinary Hospital, Tortington Lane, Arundel BN18 0BG
☎ 01903 883050
(24-hour emergency service; horses)

**Pulborough**: Arun Veterinary Group, 121 Lower Street, Pulborough RH20 2BP
☎ 01798 872089
(24-hour emergency service; dogs)

**Chichester**: Downland Veterinary Group, Stirling Lodge Clinic, 2 Stirling Road, Chichester PO19 7DJ
☎ 01243 786101
(24-hour emergency service; dogs)

**Liphook**: Liphook Equine Hospital, Home Park, Forest Mere, Liphook GU30 7JG
☎ 01428 723594 or 01428 727727
(24-hour emergency service; horses)

**Eastleigh**: Riverside Veterinary Surgery, 2 Scotter Road, Bishopstoke, Eastleigh SO50 6AJ
☎ 02380 620607
(24-hour emergency service; horses, *but* do not have 4x4 vehicles for offroad access)

**Winchester**: Stable Close Veterinary Clinic, St Cross Road, Winchester SO23 9PR
☎ 01962 840505
(24-hour emergency service; dogs)

**Stable Close Equine Practice**, Bridgets Farm, Bridgets Lane, Martyr Worthy, Winchester SO21 1AR
☎ 01962 779111
(24-hour emergency service; horses)

# Local facilities

*(S = south of the Way)*

**NB** Many post offices have shorter hours than the village shops that house them. The public phones in many villages are threatened with imminent disconnection by British Telecom. Only phones in the larger centres can be relied upon to exist/function properly.

**Eastbourne**: All facilities. Banks, places of interest, railway station, beach access.

**Birling Gap**: Pub, café, telephone, public toilets, car park, beach access, postbox, B&Bs.

**East Dean**: Pub, restaurant, shops, cafés, deli, vets, doctor, post office, telephone, postbox, Farmers Market (Wednesday am), place of interest (Sheep Centre; seasonal).

**Exceat**: Post box, café/restaurant, B&B, bike hire & accessories public toilets, visitor centre, telephone, nearby pub – The Golden Galleon.

**Seaford**: A medium-sized town with *all facilities*, including tourist information, beach access, banks, railway station, cycle shop.

**Westdean**: Telephone, forestry information board, postbox.

**Jevington**: Pub, restaurant, seasonal tea rooms, car park, telephone, postbox.

**Folkington**: Postbox.

**Wilmington**: Pub, restaurant, B&B, telephone, postbox, place of interest (Long Man of Wilmington), car park, hotel/restaurant, public toilets, tea gardens (seasonal).

**Litlington**: Pub, tea gardens, gift shop, telephone, postbox.

**Milton Street**: Pub, telephone, postbox.

**Alfriston**: Pubs, cafés, restaurants, hotels, shops, post office, postbox, book shop, telephone, car parks, public toilets, youth hostel nearby, place of interest (Clergy House).

**Berwick**: Pub, telephone, postbox.

**Alciston**: Pub, telephone, postbox.

**Selmeston**: Pub, postbox, telephone, petrol station/village store, restaurant and tea shop.

**Middle Farm**: Large farm shop, national cider centre, café, craft shop, restaurant (www.middlefarm.com).

**Firle**: Firle Place open Wednesday/Thursday/Sunday/Easter and Bank Holidays, 2–4.30pm June–September, including restaurant and teas, postbox, post office/shop, car park, blacksmith, telephone, pub. Nearby: hang gliding and paragliding centre.

**Southease**: Postbox, railway station, youth hostel (when completed).

**Rodmell**: Pub, forge and farrier, telephone, postbox, car park, place of interest (Monks House, home of Virginia Woolf).

**Iford**: Telephone, postbox.

**Kingston**: Pub, telephone, postbox.

**Newmarket**: Pub/restaurant/accommodation, postbox. Nearby petrol station/shop/café (north of A27 – cross via road bridge on Way).

**Lewes**: Historic town with *all facilities*. Banks, places of interest (castle, museum, priory), Friday Market, Farmers Market (first Saturday of month, am).

**Offham**: Pub/B&B, telephone, postbox, petrol, blacksmith, and farm shop just to north.

**East Chiltington**: Main village some distance from the Way; telephone, pub/restaurant, blacksmith, postbox.

**Plumpton**: Pub/restaurant/wi-fi, postbox.

**Westmeston**: Telephone, postbox.

**Ditchling**: Car park, pubs, public toilets, shops (incuding chemists), post office, tea rooms, place of interest, postbox, telephone, restaurants.

**Clayton**: Pub/B&B, postbox, place of interest (windmill).

**Hassocks**: *All facilities,* pubs, shops, banks, post office, public toilets, main line railway station.

**Pyecombe**: Telephone, pub, post box, saddlers/riders' supplies, 24-hour petrol station with food shop/café/toilets, ATM.

**Brighton**: Large town with *all facilities*, including backpacker hostels, railway station, places of interest.

**Saddlescombe**: National Trust information, café, campsite and toilets.

**Poynings**: Pub, post box, stained-glass workshop, garage.

**Devil's Dyke**: Pub/restaurant, public toilets and outdoor activities.

**Fulking**: Pub, telephone, postbox, spring.

**Edburton**: Smoked-salmon shop and deli (an Aladdin's cave of seafood), postbox.

**Upper Beeding**: Pubs, petrol station, shops (including chemists), postbox, Indian restaurant, post office, telephone.

**Bramber**: Pub, shops, restaurants, public toilets, hotel, place of interest (castle), telephone, postbox.

**Steyning**: Small town with *very good facilities*, public toilets, car park, shops, banks, post office, hotels, library and tourist information, cycle parts shop, Farmers Market (first Saturday of each month), doctors, vet, chemist, leisure centre, police station.

**Wiston**: Post office/store/ teas/light lunches.

**Washington**: Pub, shop, camping, telephone, B&B, postbox.

**Sullington**: Postbox, self-catering accommodation.

**Storrington**: Large village with good facilities, including hotels, B&Bs, pubs, restaurants, shops, banks, chemists, post office, telephone, petrol station (Tesco Express), library with tourist information, car park, cycle shop, Country Market (Fridays, 9.00–10.45 am).

**Arundel**: Small historic town with most facilities and castle.

**Amberley**: Pubs, hotel, restaurant, café, telephone, postbox, railway station, places of interest (museum and heritage centre; www.amberley museum.co.uk), post office, village store (some distance from the Way).

**Houghton**: Pub, telephone, postbox.

**Bury**: Pub, telephone, post office (Monday, Tuesday, Thursday afternoons), postbox, place of interest (Old Ferry Crossing).

**West Burton**: Postbox, farm shop.

**Bignor**: Telephone, postbox, place of interest (Roman villa; www.bignor romanvilla.co.uk), B&B.

**Sutton**: Pub with accommodation, postbox.

**Barlavington**: Postbox.

**Duncton**: Pub, telephone, postbox.

**Graffham**: Pubs, post office/shop, postbox, telephone, picture-framer. NB very dispersed.

**Heyshott**: Pub, telephone, postbox, farm shop.

**Cocking**: Pub, post office/shop, telephone, postbox, tea rooms (seasonal), place of interest (History Column).

**East Dean (S)**: Pub with accommodation, postbox.

**Charlton (S)**: Pub with accommodation, postbox, hotel.

**Singleton (S)**: Pub, post office in Weald and Downland Open Air Museum (www.wealddown.co.uk), shop, postbox, telephone, café/teas (sells eggs/bread/drinks), gallery.

**West Dean (S)**: Pub/restaurant, post office, shop, postbox, teas, place of interest (West Dean Gardens (restaurant/shop); www.westdean.org.uk).

**Midhurst**: Small town with *most facilities*, place of interest (house ruins). HQ of SDNP Authority.

**Bepton**: Telephone, postbox, hotel, pub (some distance from the Way).

**Didling**: Postbox.

**Treyford**: Postbox.

**Elsted**: Postbox, telephone, pub.

**East Harting**: Telephone, postbox.

**South Harting**: Post box, pubs, telephone, public toilets, post office, shop, B&Bs.

**Buriton**: Telephone, pubs, postbox.

**Chalton (S)**: Pub.

**Petersfield**: Small town with *most facilities*, railway station.

**Clanfield (S)**: Shop, restaurants, dentists, pub, telephone.

**East Meon**: Sustainability Centre (hostel, campsite with teepees and yurt, book shop, Green shop. Café (Wednesday–Sunday); www.sustainability-centre.org).

**East Meon**: Post office/shop, pubs with accommodation, cinema (last Friday of month in Village Hall), fish and chips from Izaak Walton pub (Friday night).

**West Meon**: Pubs, post office/shop/internet café, butcher/deli, telephone, pottery, postbox, smokery.

**Warnford**: Pub/B&B, postbox, telephone.

**Meonstoke, Corhampton, Exton**: Pubs, post office/shop, telephone, postbox.

**Beauworth**: Pub/B&B.

**New Cheriton**: Pub, postbox, place of interest (Hinton Ampner House and Gardens – National Trust).

**Cheriton**: Pub, post office/store, postbox.

**Chilcomb**: Postbox, telephone.

**Winchester**: Historic city with *all facilities*, railway station, places of interest, cathedral. No Youth Hostel at time of going to press.

# Local organisations

If you enjoyed your trip, you may wish to join, or contribute financially to, some of the organisations that help to conserve and manage the Downs:

**Hampshire Field Club**, Hampshire Record Office, Sussex Street, Winchester SO23 8TH
☎ 01962 846154
ⓘ www.fieldclub.hants.org.uk
(Interested in archaeology, historic buildings, landscape, local history and the New Forest.)

**Hampshire & Isle of Wight Wildlife Trust**, Beechcroft House, Vicarage Lane, Curdridge Hampshire SO32 2DP
☎ 01489 774400
✉ feedback@hwt.org.uk
ⓘ www.hwt.org.uk
(Owns and manages land of wildlife interest.)

**National Trust**, Downs Estate Office, Top Road, Slindon, Nr Arundel BN18 0RG
☎ 01243 814554

**South Downs Society**, 2 Swan Court, Station Road, Pulborough RH20 1RL
☎ 01798 875073
✉ info@southdownssociety.org.uk
ⓘ www.southdownssociety.org.uk
(Lobbies against Downland development. Keeps an eye on all rights-of-way and public access.)

**South Downs National Park Authority**, Rosemary's Parlour, North Street, Midhurst GU29 9SB
☎ 0300 303 1053
✉ info@southdowns.gov.uk
ⓘ www.southdowns.gov.uk
(Conserves and enhances the landscape, wildlife and cultural heritage of the National Park and helps people enjoy its special qualities.)

**Sussex Archaeological Society**, Bull House, 92 High Street, Lewes, East Sussex BN7 1XH
☎ 01273 486260
ⓘ www.sussexpast.co.uk
(Encourages study of local history and archaeology, and conserves historic buildings and monuments.)

**Sussex Wildlife Trust**, Woods Mill, Henfield, West Sussex BN5 9SD
☎ 01273 492630
✉ enquiries@sussexwt.org.uk
ⓘ www.sussexwt.org.uk
(Owns and manages land of wildlife interest.)

Useful Information

# Other useful addresses

**Association of Lightweight Campers**, c/o Camping and Caravanning Club, Greenfield House, Westward Way, Coventry CV4 8JH
☎ 08451 307631

**Butterfly Conservation**, Manor Yard, East Lulworth, Wareham, Dorset BH20 5QP
☎ 01929 400209
ⓘ www.butterfly-conservation.org

**British Herpetological Society** (reptiles), c/o Zoological Society, Regent's Park, London NW1 4RY

**East Sussex Reptile and Amphibian Society**, Vice-Chairman, Peter Kenward, 33 Wellington Road, Denton, Nr Newhaven, East Sussex BN9 0RD
☎ 01273 515012

**British Cycling**, National Cycling Centre, Stuart Street, Manchester M11 4DQ
☎ 0161 274 2000
ⓘ britishcycling.org.uk

**British Horse Society**, 1 Eaton House, Eaton Road, Coventry CV1 2FJ
☎ 01926 707700

**Conchological Society of Great Britain & Ireland** (snails, slugs and other molluscs), Dr Martin J. Willing, (Conservation Officer), 14 Goodwood Close, Midhurst GU29 9JG
✉ martinwilling@godalming.ac.uk

**CTC** – National Cyclist Organisation, Parklands, Railton Road, Guildford, Surrey GU2 9JX
☎ 0844 736 8450
ⓘ www.ctc.org.uk

**Farriers Registration Council**, Sefton House, Adam Court, Newark Road, Peterborough, PE1 5PP
☎ 01733 319911
ⓘ www.farrier-reg.gov.uk

**Natural England** (Headquarters), 1 East Parade, Sheffield S1 2ET
☎ 0845 600 3078
ⓘ www.naturalengland.org.uk

**Natural England** (Land Management Sussex), Guildbourne House, Chatsworth Road, Worthing BN11 1LD
☎ 0300 060 0300

**Ordnance Survey**, Adanac Drive, Southampton SO16 0AS
☎ 0845 605 0505
ⓘ www.ordnancesurvey.co.uk

**Ramblers**, Camelford House, 87/90 Albert Embankment, London SE1 7TW
☎ 020 7339 8500
ⓘ www.ramblers.org.uk
(Their annual yearbook has many bed and breakfast addresses; available free to members; available to non-members from major bookshops and newsagents.)

**Royal Society for the Protection of Birds**, The Lodge, Sandy, Bedfordshire SG19 2DL
☎ 01767 680551
ⓘ rspb.org.uk

**Sustrans**, 2 Cathedral Square, College Green, Bristol BS1 5DD
☎ 0117 926 8893
ⓘ www.sustrans.org.uk
(Promotes and builds the national cycle network and other sustainable transport initiatives.)

**Tourism South East**, 40 Chamberlayne Road, Eastleigh, Hampshire SO50 5JH.
☎ 023 8062 5400
ⓘ www.visitsoutheastengland.com

**Rural Ways**
ⓘ www.ruralways.org.uk
(Promotes sustainable tourism.)

# Guided walks

East and West Sussex, and Hampshire County Councils produce booklets of guided walks and cycle rides, many of which are on the South Downs. Contact either: The Countryside Management Service, County Hall, St Anne's Crescent, Lewes, East Sussex BN7 1UE
☎ 01273 481654
or Footprints of Sussex
ⓘ www.southdownsway.com

# Film

A film *The South Downs Way* presented by Anthony Burton is available as a download or DVD from ⓘ www.tvwalks.com

# Bibliography

Armstrong, Roy, A History of Sussex (Phillimore).

Beamish, Tufton, Battle Royal (Frederick Muller, 1965).

Brandon, Peter (ed.), The South Saxons (Phillimore).

Brandon, Peter, Sussex (Making of the English Landscape Series) (Hodder & Stoughton, 1974).

Brent, Colin, Historic Lewes and its Buildings (Lewes Town Council).

Brent, Colin, and Rector, Victorian Lewes (Phillimore, 1980).

Comber, H. (ed.), Along the South Downs Way to Winchester (with accommodation list) (Eastbourne Rambling Club, 1985).

Darby, Ben, South Downs (Hale, 1976).

Darby, Ben, View of Sussex (Hale, 1975).

Delorme, Mary, Curious Sussex (Hale, 1987).

Green, E. G., The South Downs Way (Ramblers' Association, 1970).

Harrison, David, Along the South Downs Way (Cassell, 1958).

Jebb, Miles, Guide to the South Downs Way (Constable, 1984).

Meynell, Esther, Small Talk in Sussex (Hale, 1973).

Moore, Christopher, Green Roof of Sussex (Middleton Press, 1984).

Owen, Terry, and Anderson, Peter, I Spy – What and Why on the South Downs Way (Per-Rambulations, 2010).

Parker, Mary, Riding and Road Safety Explained (Southdown Promotions, 1987).

Perkins, Ben, South Downs Walks for Motorists (Frederick Warne, 1987).

Piper, A. Cecil, Alfriston: The Story of a Sussex Downland Village (Frederick Muller, 1974).

Pyatt, E. C., Chalkways of South and South-East England (David & Charles, 1974).

Smart, Gerald, and Brandon, Peter (eds), The Future of the South Downs (Packard Publishing, 2007).

Smith & Haas, Writers in Sussex (Redcliffe, 1985).

Taylor, Rupert, The East Sussex Village Book (Countryside Books, 1986).

Teuiot, Charles, Walks along the South Downs Way (Spurbooks, 1973).

Thornton, Nicholas, Sussex Shipwrecks (Countryside Books, 1988).

Webb, Montague, Pictional Maps of the South Downs Way (Napier Publications, 1975).

Westacott, H. D., South Downs Way (Penguin, 1983).

Wills, Barclay, Bypaths in Downland (Methuen, 1927).

Youth Hostels Association, The South Downs Way (1975).

# Ordnance Survey Maps covering the South Downs Way

Explorer (1:25 000): 119, 120, 121, 122, 123, 132

Landranger (1:50 000): 185, 197, 198, 199

Motoring maps: Reach the South Downs Way using the Road 8 Travel Map

# The Official Guides to all o

## Cotswold Way
100 miles of quintessentially
English landscape

ISBN 978 1 84513 785 4

## Cleveland Way
Ian Sampson

Over 100 miles of magnificent
walking on the North York Moors

ISBN 978 1 84513 781 6

## Pennine Way
Damian Hall

The whole of England's toughest
National Trail

ISBN 978 1 84513 718 2

## Yorkshire Wolds Way
Roger Ratcliffe

A superbly tranquil walk through
the unspoilt chalk hills of Yorkshire

ISBN 978 178131 064 9

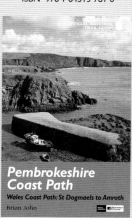

## Pembrokeshire Coast Path
Wales Coast Path: St Dogmaels to Amroth
Brian John

ISBN 978 1 84513 782 3

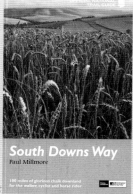

## South Downs Way
Paul Millmore

100 miles of glorious chalk downland
for the walker, cyclist and horse rider

ISBN 978 1 78131 088 5

## Hadrian's Wall Path
Anthony Burton

Follow the Roman Wall
from coast to coast

ISBN 978 1 84513 808 0

## The Ridgeway
Anthony Burton

87 miles of downland walking
from Wiltshire to the Chilterns

ISBN 978 178131 063 2

## North Downs Way
Colin Saunders

Follow the chalk ridge across South-East
England all the way to the sea

ISBN 978 178131 061 8

# ritain's National Trails

## Thames Path
### in the Country
David Sharp and Tony Gowers

From the source to Hampton Court

ISBN 978 1 84513 717 5

## Thames Path
### in London
Phoebe Clapham

From Hampton Court to Crayford Ness:
50 miles of historic riverside walk

ISBN 978 1 84513 706 9

### Peddars Way and
## Norfolk Coast Path
Bruce Robinson with Mike Robinson

90 miles from Breckland to
salt marsh and sea cliff

ISBN 978 1 84513 784 7

## South West Coast Path
### Minehead to Padstow
Roland Tarr

160 miles of coastal walking from
Exmoor to North Cornwall

ISBN 978 178131 060 1

## South West Coast Path
### Padstow to Falmouth
John Macadam

From golden beaches to rugged coves
around Britain's southernmost tip

ISBN 978 178131 062 5

## Offa's Dyke Path
### SOUTH: Chepstow to Knighton
Ernie and Kathy Kay and Mark Richards

Follow the ancient earthwork up the Wye
Valley and alongside the Black Mountains

ISBN 978 1 84513 561 4

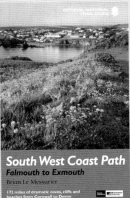

## South West Coast Path
### Falmouth to Exmouth
Brian Le Messurier

172 miles of dramatic coves, cliffs and
beaches from Cornwall to Devon

ISBN 978 1 84513 564 5

## South West Coast Path
### Exmouth to Poole
Roland Tarr

From Jane Austen's Cobb to Lulworth Cove
– over 100 miles of historic coastline

ISBN 978 178131 058 8

## OFFA'S DYKE PATH NORTH
### Knighton to Prestatyn
Ernie and Kathy Kay and Mark Richards

100 miles of walking through the
beautiful Welsh marches

ISBN 978 1 84513 312 2

## PENNINE BRIDLEWAY
### Derbyshire to the South Pennines
Sue Viccars

ISBN 1 85410 957 X

# *Other guide books from* Aurum

## The Capital Ring
Colin Saunders

78 miles of green corridor
encircling inner London

ISBN 978 1 84513 786 1

## The London Loop
David Sharp with Colin Saunders

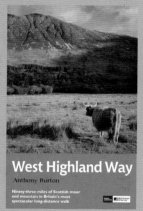

## West Highland Way
Anthony Burton

Ninety-three miles of Scottish moor
and mountain in Britain's most
spectacular long-distance walk

ISBN 978 178131 089 2

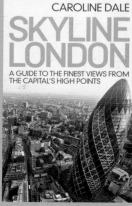

CAROLINE DALE

# SKYLINE LONDON

A GUIDE TO THE FINEST VIEWS FROM
THE CAPITAL'S HIGH POINTS

ISBN 978 1 84513 762 5

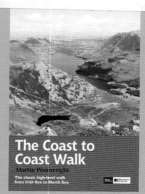

## The Coast to Coast Walk
Martin Wainwright

The classic high-level walk
from Irish Sea to North Sea

ISBN 978 1 84513 854 7